CU00692833

THE VOICE WITHIN

MY LIFE WITH SCHIZOPHRENIA

by

Lucy Adamson

Grosvenor House
Publishing Limited

This book is published by
Grosvenor House Publishing Ltd
28-30 High Street, Guildford, Surrey, GU1 3EL.
www.grosvenorhousepublishing.co.uk

A CIP record for this book
is available from the British Library

ISBN 978-1-78148-802-7

SCHIZOPHRENIA 1. Any of a group of psychotic disorders characterized by progressive deterioration of the personality, withdrawal from reality, hallucinations, emotional instability etc. **2.** Behaviour that seems to be motivated by contradictory or conflicting principles.

❊ ❊ ❊

Mention the word SCHIZOPHRENIA and the majority of people think you are talking about a violent person and someone to be avoided.

My experiences reflect the battles that many people fight in their lives and how they can be overcome. That they can hold down jobs and live a relatively 'normal' life.

It is written in an 'easy to read', understandable and accessible personal style. It is full of great stories about life on the tennis circuit and chaotic travel around the world. It has practical offerings on how to cope with voices and hallucinations, that 24 hours a day, seven days a week and three hundred and sixty five days a year, are part and parcel of everyday life for a sufferer of SCHIZOPHRENIA.

Mental health is a growing issue in the UK, with one in four adults experiencing some kind of mental health problem during a year.

❊ ❊ ❊

Chapter 1

1992, Gryfino, Poland, aged 18.

I arrived, along with T and another girl, at the airport in Berlin on route to a tennis tournament in Poland. We hired a car and set off towards Poland. We travelled through the eastern part of Berlin witnessing the difference in wealth from the western part of the city. The buildings were older and more run down and the roads cobbled and potholed. It all looked very depressing and no one looked happy. We arrived some ninety minutes later in Gryfino, a small village in North West Poland.

Gryfino had a population of approximately 20,000 inhabitants and most of them drove around in tiny Fiat 500 cars which all seemed to have seen better days and it made the place look like 'toy town'. This was my first venture into Eastern Europe and it was quite a humble place, but the people seemed to be quite hospitable and the hotel where we were staying was small and basic but quite adequate. It had to be – it was the only one in the village. The weather was grey and cold. The people seemed to be expressionless going about their daily life in Gryfino. I do not know where people worked or went to school as there was little sign of opportunity. It was about an hour to the nearest big town, Szczecin, but there was little evidence to suggest that the local population ever ventured far from their colourless community.

I was there to play a tennis tournament where I was chasing world ranking points and learning my trade as a tennis player. I was eighteen years old and this was my first real summer travelling to improve my world ranking. I had already gained some points through tournaments in England and was ranked a very modest 900 in the world, which was not enough to gain me direct acceptance into the main draw of the tournament, and meant that I had to battle through an 'open' qualifying event of 128 players. This meant that the four elusive qualifier places in the main event had to be won by competing in the qualifying and having to win five consecutive rounds of matches in order to just get into the main draw. Qualification was my aim as world ranking points and prize money were only on offer once you competed in the main draw proper. Both of these incentives spurred on all the players making it a highly competitive arena. The prize money for the tournament was $10,000 which may sound a lot, but this was split between all main draw singles and doubles competitors with the main first prize not amounting to much more that $1200. This doesn't stretch very far when you have travel and accommodation living expenses to cater for. I was making a financial loss!

It was the summer of 1992 in my summer break from Loughborough University where I was studying psychology. I was travelling with another British player — She was similarly ranked to me although was older and had been playing at this level for a bit longer. She coached in her spare time back in England and was pleased to travel with me to these overseas events as most of her experience had been gained through playing a similar level of event in England. I had met her at one of these home events and had played doubles with her on a few occasions. She was quite laid back and didn't like practising which at first I found difficult as I was a bit of a practice addict. I wanted to be on court at every spare moment – I tended to leave my best tennis on the practice court where there is no pressure and no money or ranking points at stake. My travelling companion preferred the 'real thing' and was probably a better competitor than me. She had a similar ranking so we were both in a similar situation regarding having to qualify before any real gains were made.

We had already had three weeks in Belgium where the results had been less than noteworthy. I had played a Yugoslavian girl. In the first event, who was very powerful and the whole experience seemed to rush by me before I had really settled in. I did not qualify for the main event so was disappointed and had had my confidence knocked by watching players at this level competing for their living. The other two events also saw me lose my first matches.

I felt that I was not really good enough to be there but on the other hand felt excited to be part of such a competitive sport, after all I had been playing for the last ten years to get towards this sort of situation. I never thought I would be in this environment despite working hard at my tennis for years. I always knew I enjoyed playing and competing but never really believed it was something that I could do on an international stage.

My confidence was beginning to dwindle. With a ranking of 900 and the fact that I was not winning a first round match I began to realise there were hundreds of girls out there capable of playing better tennis than me. Players came from all over Europe mainly, although there were a few South Americans coming over to Europe to play on the slow clay courts that they are so familiar with in their native countries. This was one of my first trips abroad to play tennis and for me it was a learning experience but it was looking to be steep learning curve. Many things were new to me, I was beginning to see the depth in the game with many players all striving towards the goal of getting ranking points. I was learning the system and procedure of what was required to compete. Entries for the events were done prior to leaving home but it was still a necessity to sign in when arriving at the tournament site. The draw was then done after the sign in had closed and players would linger about waiting to see who they would be drawn to play against. Then the order of play would be published determining what time you would play the next day and when you knew that then you could fight for booking a practice court at an appropriate time prior to your match time. With so many players scrabbling over limited practice facilities this was 'a dog eat dog' experience that had to be learned on the hoof. Many of the other competitors seemed to be a lot tougher at this that I was and again I struggled with asserting myself in these situations where I felt I did not quite fit in. It had to be done though, so I guess I learned to push myself forwards on a daily basis in order to give myself the best chance to play well.

We had been in Gryfino for a couple of days practising when match day arrived – I was dreading it as all my confidence had gone seeing all these other girls practicing and looking much more competent than me.

All the courts at the tennis centre are close together so it was possible to sit around and watch everyone practice. One of my first impressions was the athleticism of many of the girls and their desire to compete. I know I wanted to compete but again I felt slightly in awe of the other girls. I assumed that they were hardened competitors who knew the ropes better than I did. I avoided watching them if at all possible as I knew I was beginning to struggle with the environment. Watching the other players I found quite intimidating as I was forever questioning my right to be there. I was drawn to play a Czech girl called Vera Vlaçkova – I didn't know her, another faceless Eastern European.

My match was called on a damp heavy day in grey Gryfino. Rain was in the air and the village looked even less inviting than it had done the previous day. The buildings matched the people in their monochrome bleak nature. It was cold and I was not looking forward to playing on the soft clay courts which were conducive to a patient slow game which I felt incapable of on this particular day. I was feeling aggravated and felt that if someone said one wrong word to me I would snap back. In reality, this is not my way of operating. I am non confrontational and will walk away in silence consuming any irritation I may feel inside of me. The weather just added to my crabbiness. I am a warm weather person and love to play with the sun on my back. Gryfino on this given day could not be further from such an ideal.

The match was called by the Referee and I went to the court and found this girl with two rackets and holey shoes and unmatched tennis clothes in various shades of grey. I walked on to court with a racket bag full of rackets, matching kit and new shoes looking the part of a full time tennis player. I think I presented the picture of a confident player with all the clothes and equipment. I always took pride in how I looked on the court as I know in the past I had been intimidated by that players seeming to be in control and having everything. A lot of promising players receive rackets and clothing from suppliers free. I thought that if players were provided with all the equipment and clothing someone must be backing them to use and wear their brands. This in turn must mean that they are worth backing and must have performed to a good standard. Although I was in the situation of looking the part I knew that the clothes had come from another player as had the rackets – I was just lucky to have connections in this instance. If it had been me walking on the court facing someone turned out like me I would have noticed. Vlaçkova however seemed unfazed.

My thinking was that if she can get there without anything she must be able to play tennis – I had been given everything and had no right to be there – I had never proved myself on the tennis courts. Nerves overtook me. I started to warm up and Vlaçkova was quite consistent but it was difficult to read her style of play in the knock up. It was difficult to determine how good she was as she warmed up in a very controlled manner without much exertion. She seemed to be competent but not outstanding in all aspects of her game and I was beginning to be intimidated not being able to form an impression in my mind as to how to oppose Vlaçkova. I was looking for an easy answer so I didn't really have to compete but would win without much application. I was afraid to give it everything because if I did that and then lost it would reflect on my lack of competence. What would that look like losing to another Eastern European tennis player. Vlaçkova was one of many churned out each year in a similar mould. No emotions on show just a quiet competent determination to make something of themselves. The match started and I fell apart.

I am frozen with nerves, the first two games slip away due to being paralysed with nerves and a total melt down of confidence. There is a male aggressive voice in my head shouting that the Polish police are going to kill me. I am petrified. I had heard voices before but never threatening and was previously of the belief that everyone has episodes like where a voice follows you around for periods of time commentating on what you do. I had never experienced anything like what was to follow during the fated match with Vlackova.

Usually for me the tennis court has provided a solace for me. It has always been a place where I go into my own world with no one else interfering on my side of the court – I can just get on and do my business in peace. Quite often in a match situation I would imagine myself in a glass box where if there were people watching they would be safely out of my range and any noise that they generated would be muffled by the walls – I was, as I say, in my own world. Today was different. Someone (a voice now known to me as Arthur) had broken into my glass box and was shouting at me in a threatening voice that the Polish police wanted to kill me over and over again. The spaces between points that are usually a haven for me had become a torrent of abuse and hatred from this male voice. I knew I must have done something very bad and must be a bad person to the core to warrant such vitriol. My fear escalated and the tennis passed very quickly into an easy loss against the girl with two rackets from the Czech Republic.

As petrified as I was, there was no one to whom I could possibly mention what had happened on the court as my life was in jeopardy – they were waiting for me in order to kill me. I walked up the stairs to the dressing room in tears and the Polish men chanted her name over and over again – Vlaçkova, Vlaçkova, Vlaçkova. To this day I know not if that was Arthur (the voice) or the real Polish people, again though it put the fear of God into me.

In the dressing room the men were there again – following me like the voices had previously – Vlaçkova, Vlaçkova, Vlaçkova. These men were in the ladies dressing room as real as they come and very intimidating and frightening. The voices were telling me that the police wanted to kill me and men were following me into the dressing room. This was the beginning of things to come – hearing things, seeing things – the beginning of the rest of my life.

This was my first real experience with Arthur as an aggressive voice. I was so threatened by him that there was no question of me talking to anyone about him. His presence was continuous although not always loud the voice was always menacing. No longer the ineffectual commentary on my life, but definite threats to my safety suggesting that someone out there wanted to kill me. I didn't know who it was to be so I had to be on guard all of the time and also to keep away from people.

All through the following weeks, another two in Poland and then two in Bulgaria, I found I was isolating myself and my new fear, as it was too risky to speak to anyone.

I felt that if any one knew, they may be on Arthur's side and may be the person out there who would kill me. Also I thought that I must be a really bad person if someone wanted to kill me and if that was the case I did not want anyone to know me. I felt as if people knew what I was thinking, knew that I was in a dangerous position, yet the most dangerous thing would have been for them to actually know – that would be the death of me. With people coming close to me I couldn't let them in so I avoided as much contact as possible to revert to my own problems alone. Isolation.

Tennis was no longer a solace as the glass box, which had previously allowed me to hold it together playing in front of people, had been violated. Once violated it has never been the same since – not one moment of peace anymore. Tennis that summer became a stage where I was totally exposed and at risk. I still had people out to kill me even when I made it out of Poland into Bulgaria.

Arthur was haunting, taunting and dominating my life, from that day forever.

Arthur continued to follow me around 24/7 and this experience was to be the end of any freedom that I had in my mind and in my life. By commentating on my every move it is difficult to dispute that people are watching me – they know everything that goes on with me I am never safe. I have concerns that as a result of being watched all the time I am going to do something desperate to myself in order to silence the voices, but somehow I believe the voices will come with me. There is to be no peace. I feel that for some reason I deserve this situation – I must have done something very wrong for this situation to have occurred, basically I am a bad person who is rotten at the core – the core of me is dominated by voices that can only be telling the truth – why else would they be so aggressive about the message that someone will kill me?

One day I believe I will find out but when the voices began to taunt part of me died anyway.

I wonder whether the stress of the event, the pressure I placed upon myself to do well, along with the lack of contact I kept with the outside world when I travelled on my tennis escapades – I never phoned home or attempted to communicate. I don't know if that was a conscious decision or just another part of my protective isolation – the less I talked the less people would know about me. It seemed that most people knew my thoughts anyway and I was ashamed of them as they were so negative.

On many occasions the thought to end it all had more than crossed my mind although no action had been taken – I was too weak for that. I do remember asking other people how they would kill themselves if it ever came to it. The response was polite avoidance of the question. I had decided if ever I was going to kill myself it would be to jump off a tall building as I was afraid of heights and if that fear put me off jumping then I wasn't ready to jump. In months to come more cowardly methods appeared more appealing but here I am telling the tale.

Chapter 2

One of my earliest memories is one that sticks in my mind. It may not be the earliest, but it is one I recall quite clearly. My next door neighbour at the time was a boy that I played with some times. One afternoon he came round to play but I did not want to. When he did not go away I got the carving knife out of the kitchen and proceeded to chase him around the garden whilst brandishing it! Before I managed to catch my victim my eldest brother came out from the house and stopped the chase. I do not know what I would have done if I had caught my friend but I wasn't bothered by him wanting to come round to play for some time after the event!!

'Did you have a happy childhood?' is a false question. As a child I did not know what happiness was, and whether I was happy or not, I was too busy being.' *Alistair Reid.*

From the age of about 6 or 7 onwards I had four parents. My Mum and Dad found better company in the presence of another couple who would eventually switch partners to become my four parents. Before the official swapping date (which I cannot clearly recall), I used to spend weekends with my Dad and his current wife at her house with her sons. I was a school year younger than her youngest, which I thought was great, as now I had a tenuous link with the 'in crowd' in the year above! These weekends changed however when during a painting and drawing session on a weekend with my Dad and his now wife he announced that he wouldn't be coming home any more and that he was going to live with Pat. I was devastated and remember being in floods of tears - why did they have to change an arrangement which according to my young eyes was the best of both worlds? Why did he need another woman when he had me?

Weekends changed but I still spent time at my Dads and saw a lot of him as he still lived in the same village. In the mean time John had moved in with my mother. I do not remember the exact change over or how he became part of the household. I recall staying with my Dad at weekends and becoming very attached to him and not wanting to go home to my Mum on a Sunday evening. My Dad would take me back to my Mums but I would sit in the car and cry. I guess I didn't want to let go although it must have been difficult for all involved at the time. Also I used to be the same when my Dad went abroad on business, I would cling on and be very upset if he had to go. I was quite young when this happened and all my reactions were without thought as to how they may affect others and I am unaware as to how my three older brothers dealt with the situation. Every Friday I would ring my Dad and we would go to the village Sports and Social Club to play the fruit machines and video games which I really enjoyed. I would drink ginger beer and be treated to a bar of chocolate which I always looked forward to. One week however, I broke my arm at school so when I rang Dad to arrange our evening out I asked if he could pick me up. He told me to cycle round but I couldn't tell him about my arm so decided to walk around to his house (only 5 minutes away). I did not want any possible reason for him not to want me. When he saw me he said why didn't I tell him, but again for some reason I was embarrassed at being damaged and could not tell him. This was to be a pattern that lasted through my life. Holidays were taken together. I would spend some time in the summer, usually in Cornwall (although we did branch out further a field when I was a bit older) where I would spend some time with Dad and Pat and some time with Mum and John. These holidays were enjoyed greatly despite consisting of long periods of surfing in the freezing sea (which we appeared to be immune to) and eating sandy sandwiches (which we also appeared to be immune to!). By the time I was 11 or 12 however tennis had taken over my life and the family holidays were kicked into touch.

My mother is a very independent character who worked until her retirement at 60. She went to University and has a degree in Chemistry. She is also a very loyal person who has, although not always smoothly, supported my choices and respected my decisions even though at times they didn't coincide with hers! She is a very egalitarian person who has an acceptance of people regardless of their social, race or ethnic status. Our family has become very cosmopolitan with two of my brothers marrying Asians – one is Japanese and one Thai. At other periods of time we were all out of the country with my eldest brother living with his wife in New York and Steve and Rick travelling or settling on the other side of the world. I myself was at the time travelling pursuing my tennis interest and as I will describe later I was quite remiss at keeping in touch. Despite these disparate years we are close to each other now and communication in our family, via Mum, has been much improved. Mum, however, has not always, in my mind, appeared to accept my illness. Being a person with quite a positive outlook I feel that she believes in minimising any presenting problems. This may be fine sometimes but at others it is more comfortable for problems to be acknowledged and an attempt made to understand. By saying 'oh but you look so well' it doesn't necessarily remove the problem (which may be an unrealistic dream of mine, I accept). I do not believe I have ever heard my Mum mention the word 'schizophrenia', and I know that labels are not always helpful but sometimes the acceptance of it is important for me. It makes it quite embarrassing to feel that I suffer from something that my mother can not even mention the name of! This in turn can make it difficult to talk about my set backs but over time I feel that we are getting closer to my desired acceptance.

John who married my Mum, as her second husband over 25 years ago, hails from the north of the country and is proud of his northern traditional roots. He is caring to a fault and has always been there for me when I probably haven't been the most communicative of people. In his later years John has become more open and able to accept a wider viewpoint on many aspects – a quality that my mother encouraged in him. He has shown his flexibility by adopting a late career change into IT teaching after a long period of time working as a successful civil engineer which quite rightly he should be proud of. Today John is a sufferer of Parkinson's Disease but in my eyes his has made him a more adaptable person. He is still fairly rigid but is rebuilding his life around an illness that knocked him off his feet at the original diagnosis. I will always look after him.

Dad is completely different and is quite a competitive, driven man who is quite achievement orientated. He also went to University and got a first class degree in Chemistry. His ambitions saw him fair well in his academic life early on and then saw a lifelong career in pharmaceuticals which absorbed his time significantly. He had time however to pursue various sports including table tennis and cricket and in later years an addiction to golf. This sporting side to his persona is one that I can relate to and admire his drive to achieve. Somehow however I feel that I probably tried too hard to emulate his successes and never really felt I achieved on a similar broad range of his work and leisure spectrum. It was only when I married that I felt that the need to live up to family expectations was lifted from my shoulders and I could begin to relax a bit more in my life.

I do not place blame on anyone for this aspect of my life as it has always been within my control to mediate my choices of what and how to pursue goals in my life. Dad has a very scientific approach to my illness and looks for factual causes and cures. When he was invited to speak to my therapist and psychiatrist and found out that schizophrenia was what I was dealing with he made it his mission to understand the problem. On seeing an advert in the daily papers for a talk on schizophrenia he immediately asked if I would like to go with him. I was apprehensive but did go and his interest in the subject was valued by me. From this he learnt that using recreational drugs such as cannabis can lead to schizophrenia and I even managed to hold a discussion with him about cannabis use and how although I had used it fairly regularly for a while when I was at school I did not believe it added to my symptoms. Prior to our trip to London for this talk and his involvement with Annie my therapist, these topics of conversation would have been totally off the agenda. Dad is also interested in the medication that I take and the factual side of the illness, but when it comes to emotional aspects that I experience I find it very difficult to get past my own inhibitions to speak to him about this.

The final piece of the parental jigsaw is Pat – my Dad's second wife and the ex wife of John. Pat is a great social animal who partakes greatly in the village activities and golf club etc. Pat is the talkative one in the family always coming up with conversation which compliments my Dad as he is the quieter of the two. Pat is very inclusive and is always in contact with me and I believe encourages Dad to pick up the phone when I am just as bad and haven't communicated for a while. I feel that Pat's three sons are a lot closer communicatively than the siblings on my side of the family although my brothers and I are all close in feelings if not words.

Being the youngest of four siblings, three elder brothers who were ten, eight and six years older than me respectively, gave me the challenge to grow up and stand my ground. My brothers were always caring for me indifferent ways but I still wanted to be that bit older to be more involved in their lives, especially Ed, the eldest.

It was with Ed that I felt the most distant because of the age gap and differences in school life etc. Rick lived at home until a later age so there was a period when there was just him and me living at home so we got on quite well then. Steve the youngest, always played rough games with me such as wrestling and boxing with cushions in the lounge! This was the normal bit of my childhood.

Being the youngest of four it was important to grow up quickly. My life as a tennis player took over when I was 8 years old which again demanded time and application, forgoing weekends or sleepovers with friends as I would rather be practicing or competing on the tennis scene. This would continue to grow and develop over time and the nature of the game demands a lot of time and an outlook beyond ones years in the early days. How many kids give up evenings and weekends to play tennis every weekend and every holiday. I stopped going on the traditional summer holiday with my Dad when I was 11 years old as there were more important competitive events in the form of the National Championships down in Eastbourne for all of the best juniors in the country. I could not afford two weeks in the sun with my Dad before this, as I needed to prepare. After a year long commitment of tournaments and practice, it was not an option to arrive at the tournament not having played for two weeks. These circumstances may not have been representative of a 'normal' childhood, and I feel I had left my child within even at the tender age of 12.

When I first entered therapy I had to complete an 'origins of my family' questionnaire in which I was allowed to use one word to describe family members – my choice of word for Ed was 'aloof'. This word was chosen because I felt I could connect with Ed in shared aloofness even though that may not be the way others saw either of us.

Because of our age gap and the apartness of Ed's nature when we were growing up my memories of this period of time are sparse and rather anecdotal.

An incident that I recall is when I was racing Steve on our bikes on the road and we clipped wheels and I went over the handlebars cutting my head. Mum was at work and no one else was at home with the exception of Ed who was studying in the dining room. Steve told me to go to Ed and ask him what to do with this cut. I was nervous about interrupting Ed, which had nothing to do with Ed but more to do with the fact that I hated showing any weakness or neediness. I asked him what to do and he proceeded to get some surgical spirit and cotton wool to bathe the cut which stung like hell. He seemed to be inpatient with my complaints but that was how I remember him to be. Very self sufficient and with short shrift for those who did not match his standards. These were standards which I very much wanted to emulate. I later realised that this air of Ed's was not as formidable as it seemed. Underneath is a caring warm person who has many qualities not necessarily seen by enough people.

Ed was always very knowledgeable and academic, seeming to have a wide grasp of current affairs swotted up on his paper round which he did reading the papers as he delivered. He was academically a high achiever, as would be expected from someone with such high personal standards, and I always wanted to emulate that. I felt if I was going to get into Ed's world I would have to be bright enough to be worth while in his mind. Now when I think about this I realise that his judgements of people are not so shallow, but none the less I feel that if I achieve Ed is always there to recognise the efforts. This recognition is cherished. Ed also achieved on a musical front and I recall him travelling to the USA with a local musical theatre group. He returned home with a pair of red dungarees which I wanted and I remember trying them on when he had put them in the washing basket in the bathroom but alas they were a few sizes too big. I have not forgotten them though and still hold a soft spot for bright red dungarees!

Ed and some of his friends formed a rock group called the 'Turkeys' which I was very proud of. He sprayed the name of his band on a sheet with purple spray paint as the backdrop for his gigs (I do not know if these ever took place). I felt very important telling my friends at school that my brother was in a rock band! Ed used to occupy a bedroom downstairs at home which I thought would be great as you wouldn't have to bother with the stairs, and he had a drum kit in his bedroom which was hammered to death on many occasions. I did not mind however as it was part of him being different and having the confidence to be different which I craved.

Ed's friends also attracted my attention with their striped trousers and blue eyeliner. Ed had his ear pierced and I remember him hanging a miniature teaspoon from it.

It was this individualism which appealed and I felt that I would always follow him as I felt a bit different myself. I could not define this different feeling but I knew that I was not going to be the Girl Guide type which most of my friends in the village became. It seemed that Ed did not need anyone and did not like many people which was exactly how I felt – Ed was my idol and if he did not need people then nor did I!

Ed went away to university in Brighton with a year in the States which again I felt was an achievement and made Ed special. Talking to friends who had siblings at university I felt Ed was a cut above as he was in the US. As my family was fairly academic it was taken for granted in my mind that everyone went to university. One day I would do the same and would strive for the independence which made Ed the brother that he was.

After university I remember a time that Ed was in Barcelona working. This was another achievement and when I went to Barcelona, with a group of juniors and a coach, to play tennis I felt so excited that Ed would come to see me. He did not really know too much about my tennis life and I was only 14 so it was probably a bit of a drag to come and visit his little sister but it meant a lot to me to see him there. It was a difficult week of tennis with me arguing a lot with my coach, but to have Ed visit made the week bearable.

I did not really keep much contact with Ed whilst he was abroad and felt we had kind of grown apart even though we had not really been very close beforehand. Even when Ed came back to London things did not go too smoothly.

I remember meeting Ed just before Christmas one year with Mum in London. After half an hour of difficult chat Mum asked Ed about Christmas and he did not answer. She asked what the matter was and he replied that he 'did not do idle chit chat!' This summed it up at the time and it was really difficult to break into his world. At this time however I became more determined that I wanted to be like Ed and set about not doing idle chit chat myself. I do not think I mastered it to the extent that Ed did but it was something that I strove to include in my repertoire – silence.

As far as I was aware Ed had been seeing B on and off for a period of time. It was difficult to gauge how close they were as Ed did not offer information freely. When Ed met Mum and I in London and announced the news that he was to marry B we were both shocked and over the moon. It was a great feeling to see Ed smile as it was an expression that was kept hidden on many occasions. I did not really know B and the wedding was quite a daunting proposition for me. I was already struggling with depression although I do not think I had been diagnosed as schizophrenic the symptoms were very much present. The thought of spending a day doing idle chit chat with family and unknown others filled me with dread although I wanted to be there for Ed. I took a friend as T was away and we stayed for the ceremony and the lunch which I only remember for Ed's speech which was fantastic and B and Ed who both looked amazing. I did not really know B then but spoke to her briefly just to apologize for leaving so early. I could not stay for the evening party as people just scared me too much and it was all too overwhelming. This is one thing that I regret to this day and it is on my list of things that

I would love to have the chance to do all over again and a whole lot differently.

After Ed and B were married they invited me around to dinner. I was so excited and nervous at the same time but I had the best time I could remember. T dropped me off at their place in Finsbury Park and I stayed for dinner before being collected again. I was worried about Ed's opinion of T so kept them apart which now I realise was totally unnecessary. During the dinner I saw a side of Ed that I had never experienced before. Relaxed and funny he was great company which served yet again as a source of admiration that I wished to emulate in myself – such assuredness. Also I began to get to know B which has been one of the most important things I have done in my life. She was warm, honest and open and although I was someone new in her life I felt accepted for who I was and did not have to be anything special. This experience of the three of us together was to prove to be the catalyst for many developments in my life in later months.

Rick is my middle brother who is married to Tomoko (a very outgoing Japanese treasure) and has three gorgeous kids – Jake (8), Molly (5) and Scott. Rick is a bit more reserved and doesn't show his feelings easily, rather like Dad. I feel bad that I am not able to recall the time and care that Rick showed to me when I was his baby sister. Apparently when I was young Rick used to play with me and look after me with great fondness. I feel guilty now that I cannot recall those days; but I do believe the stories I have heard of his time spent with me. If it was anything like the time he spends with his own children then I was very lucky. Rick, today, would never admit it to me, or to anyone, how he used to look after his little sister.

He is man of little emotion and few words. He is a very proud person who has a beautiful family and great family values. They are all totally relaxed and do not have a materialistic thought or need. There is no lack of affection but it is always done in a very male way by Rick. Tomoko is a very outgoing person, in contrast, which makes for a great partnership and I am glad to be part of the same family. Rick runs what appears to be a successful small building business in Cambridge. He never talks about it so I can only assume it is doing okay. Tomoko has spent the last few years raising the children and it is only recently since Molly started school that she has regained some time to herself. This time of more child free moments has not been reached with a sigh of relief, as Tomoko loves having them at home and school is just a bit of an inconvenience.

Jake is now 8 years old and is a gem. He looks fantastic with straight Asian hair and dark brown eyes. His skin is slightly tanned and oriental but his smile is that of a sun ray. His mind is like a sponge and his grasp of ideas is way beyond his years. He appears to be 8 going on 30.

Molly aged 5 is becoming equally adept on the chatting front and it is patently obvious that this comes from Tomoko's outgoing demeanour rather than Rick's quieter exterior.

I do not even know if Rick knows about my illness! It is never talked about and he never asks questions which is again fine with me as we have a completely different relationship to that which I share with Ed and B. Rick is a reliable brother who would always be there for any of our family, (as would Ed and Steve). He would never let me know that in words but it is a feeling of reliance and trust I experience while being with Rick and his family. Despite this caring side he remains a part more of my father's side of the family because there must be secrets inside that will probably never be spoken about.

Finally there is Steve and Ding with their two girls Gwen and Maggie. They live in Bangkok, Thailand, which is Ding's home country, and are one of the most relaxed families I know who show their love for the girls in abundance. As they live miles away contact is by email and the occasional chat on the phone. Steve and his family have been lucky enough to come back to the UK to visit for the last few summers and the contact is great. Steve always surprises me in his achievements as he always plays himself down but does so well for himself. I see some of me in him as he is always keen to learn. This is something that runs strongly through my veins as well. Somehow, despite the chaos that Steve and Ding live in, Steve managed to study for a MSc recently which he was awarded – what a fantastic achievement. Steve has always been positive for me and very encouraging albeit from a distance. Steve always reassures me that it can be done – whatever it is. Steve does know that I struggle but I haven't really told him any details of what is going on for me. I think he has talked with Mum about it and then we have strange conversations in which we both assume that the other knows what we are talking about! If I needed to however, I feel I could speak to Steve about anything. The trust is there and he is a very caring human person.

Steve was the one who used to take me to primary school in the next village on the bus. At first I did not want to go and cried and cried not letting Steve leave me. Then it would be morning assembly where Steve would be sitting on the opposite side of the hall. I would sit through the assembly trying to cut myself to draw blood so that I could then go and ask Steve to help me make it better. I cannot remember when I felt safe enough not to do that anymore but soon I settled down to school but it was not my favourite way to spend my time.

The final member of my family is T. He became an important member when I was just 14.

He has been pivotal in my battle against the demons. He has been a constant factor throughout the good times and the bad, but has never faltered in his commitment to saving me.

I met T when I was 14 years old and he immediately had an impact on my life! He appeared when I was playing a tennis match at Devonshire Park in Eastbourne. For me it was not just another tennis match, but a chance to justify my ability to the powers that be in the game. It was the National Grass Court Championships where all the best players aged 14 and under compete. The top 48 in the country are accepted into the event, and on this occasion I was seeded number 5. Supposedly the fifth best player in the draw. In the first round I was displaying my usual 'hot and cold' tennis – a model of inconsistencies, when this man, watching whilst sitting on a bin outside the corner of the court, started to tell me what to do! For some unfathomable reason I started to listen to him and his instructions. From 1-4 down in the third deciding set, I managed to win it 6-4. I went to seek out this man after the match – little did I know that he would be my saviour on many occasions in my life that were far more important than a junior tennis match. We chatted for ages about all sorts of topics and immediately hit it off. He made sense to me; and more importantly at that same time gave my tennis a sense of purpose – a new vein of life. T supported me all through my matches that week and discussed them with me afterwards. This became a pattern through my tennis life.

This man had more to offer me than being a tennis guru though. Instantly our personalities clicked - not instant love, but it was an instant friendship. When Eastbourne came to an end in the quarterfinals we went our separate ways. I was content, with a new direction and vision, in my tennis life, and more importantly with a new friend.

We met quite frequently at tennis events and immediately clicked back into a comfortable friendship – little did we know about what the future held in store for us, and what our future would be like together.

T was always there for me at the end of the phone. Occasionally we would meet, but for ages tennis was our motivation, and our friendship developed around this common passion that we shared. This compatibility made sure our relationship flourished, and even from a distance the connection never faltered. I would ring T some evenings when I was home alone and we would talk until Mum returned home from her evening work.

Our friendship continued for the next three to four years where seeing each other was limited but took place at tennis events where T and I had an excuse to be there. Otherwise connection was just via the telephone. These days T hates to talk on the phone so I think we did well to build well to build our friendship this way.

Things were not always plain sailing – there was a large age gap (which although never a problem to us did seem to be a hurdle for others on the outside). Our budding love had to be confined to clandestine meetings and telephone calls when life seemed to be full of people that could not see the connection that I was experiencing and enjoying. To have that commitment and fun for me was intoxicating. The clandestine meetings added spice to an already highly flavoured cocktail. This continued throughout university, and then through many more ups and downs such as Madras General Hospital and numerous back operations, ECT and in patient psychiatric spells where the pervasive feeling from others was that it would not last. Determination, though, is a hidden quality of mine and also T. He wears his heart on his sleeve and you could never doubt his 110% commitment to me.

I never planned marriage. I did not think we needed it. Occasionally I would joke about it but for me T's love was enough. In 2004 things changed. I was well enough to realise what T had put himself through for me. Good and bad; and there was plenty of bad ranging from attempted overdoses to slashing arms and wrists with razor blades. I did these things to hurt myself and never registered how much I must have been hurting T and those around me. We stuck it out. I became more stable and we talked more about marriage and disappearing to Las Vegas or Florida to tie the knot. We became so serious that at dinner one night with one of T's best friends, David, we told him of our plans. 'Rubbish' he said taking us aback as he had always supported us. David then followed it up by saying that he for one wanted to be there as did Janice his wife and Amanda his daughter. We must do it in England so our friends can be part of it. We thought again and started listing people we wanted to be there. Eventually we had a plan of a family only registry office service and a celebration lunch for our closest 30 friends at a great venue afterwards. It was welcomed by all, for by this time we had long been accepted as a couple even if it was just for our staying power and defiance of all that came up against us! We had strength.

Martin was our natural choice to be best man on our wedding day. He is T's closest friend and has been for over 30 years. T is almost part of Janet and Martin's family. Both Janet and Martin are keen tennis players representing the County at various levels. Janet also captained the Ladies County team for Hertfordshire.

We often find ourselves together, putting the tennis world to rights over a bottle of red and a Chinese takeaway. It goes without saying that they would be important people on our special day.

The Day was fantastic. Martin, our Best Man, and Janet, collected us in the morning and they did it in style. They had promised us their own car decorated but they arrived with a white Rolls Royce that they had secretly arranged for us. The day was going to be good! It was fantastic. It was October 18, 2004; one of the most important and special days that I have lived through.

I never thought it would make much difference, but now I was Mrs Adamson for all to see. It cemented and made public what we always knew we had, but now our commitment was there for all to see. Our love has never been in question, and has continued to grow everyday. This has kept me going through desperate times and encourages me to go forth in times of doubt. I have never doubted T. Only myself! I have enough love in my body from T to fulfil all my dreams I have ever had, it is hard to describe but is never hidden away. I am proud to be Mrs Adamson even if some days I am not proud to be myself. I love T whereas self love has been a lot harder to come by.

I have been lucky enough to have people around me who love me. T is the obvious candidate for this, but one man I idolised from my young days also helped enormously. My brother, Ed, an enigma to me, encouraged me to spread my love firstly to welcome his wife B and himself Ed into my life in a bigger role, and from then introducing ourselves back into the family unit. We had always been fairly independent free spirits from our family and never really shared those deep inner feelings as relationships, although never negative they were sometimes guarded. In our nights in New York City on Ed and B's roof terrace we would discuss our secrets, concerns, worries and loves. We became close and promised never to let that go. We haven't. Also through this rooftop therapy and my time with Annie and Dr R, I have re-evaluated the strength of our family – especially my relationship with my parents. Mum has become another key person in my life. We are honest and open with each other and share more of our ups and downs. We socialise together, play tennis together, shop together and most of all speak to each other on a daily basis. Nothing earth shattering but re-affirmation that we are there for each other. I thank Ed and B for this as it was their strength and commitment to the family that gave me the courage to open up and talk. Freed from the veil of secrecy, which was prominent in so many facets of my younger years. Free to be myself once more.

This love, pervasive throughout my life today provides me with the self worth, fragile as it may be, to go on and thrive. I try to tackle new obstacles and to battle the old foes. Without love I would not be here today, that is certain, and the flagship of my love will always be T. Our marriage was a big day for me and I know inside that I became someone that day which may sound dramatic but it was a huge shift for my belief. I was wanted, needed and accepted by all the most important people in my life. I can now fight my battles with a vision that was missing before – and I am winning. I may not wear my determination on my sleeve as my husband does - but it is a solid core within me. We will survive.

Chapter 3

When I was 5 years old I started at primary school in the next village. I do not remember my first day but I do remember the early days when Steve would travel with me on the bus and deliver me to my classroom. He was in the senior class so used to go off to his room when he had delivered me. This sounds straight forward but I did not like being left at school and Steve had to do this on a daily basis. I would arrive in my reception class and the tears would start. I would not let him leave. I guess at some stage I would get distracted and he would sneak out but I do recall this feeling of being left. It was a feeling I did not like. Following the register the whole school would file into the school hall for an assembly. Steve would be there as well with his class in a different area of the hall and then all the emotions were brought up again. I would sit through assembly scheming as to how I could spend time with Steve. My solution was to cut myself, or scratch myself until the skin broke and blood was drawn. This way, at the end of the assembly I could go to the teacher and tell them I needed Steve to help me. This did not really work as he was never allowed to, but I remember the process quite clearly. This was my child. I was lonely, yet in a crowd of children, desperate to escape and fearful of being left at every moment of time. I have cut myself, which I enjoy doing at times, as a huge release of tension is experienced. It is no longer done to get the attention of a loved one as it is something very private to me and has a negative stigma with it and I do not wish to be seen as weak. There are many times when I wish I could do it freely-the results are very intoxicating. Today I have a cigarette to try to get the same buzz. Both methods are supposedly harmful to you, but both make you feel good in different ways.

The feeling of being lonely in a crowd of people is a common feeling today. If I go to a party or out with a group of friends, if the group is too large (5 or 6), I feel at a loss and am not sure how to be. I therefore shut down and feel the isolation within the group. Maybe because this has been done for so many years it will be a tough one to change. The need to escape, sometimes leading to the verge of panic is a feeling that I largely experience at work. I know I cannot afford to expose any weakness at work though so put on an act in order to cope. If I let my guard down or overload myself then life is hard to keep control over.

These patterns were visible when I was 5 years old in a different time phase and emotional awareness. The patterns recur though. This was brought to my attention during a discussion with my counselling supervisor which shows that I do have an awareness of my child within as I still replicate the feelings. It need not be an overt display but the fact it is happening proves that I am not the hollow individual that sometimes I feel.

It was when I was at primary school that I started to play tennis and was so keen that I always took a racket and ball to school and played against the wall. This started a craze which I was very happy about as it was a craze that I was good at. Also I started to run competitions in the school hall for the kids in the younger years to play mini tennis during their break times. I would organise competitions and provide chocolate bars as prizes which seemed to go down well. This represented the early days of my love for tennis.

I was in a mixed age group year at primary school with me being in the younger of the two combined years. At the end of my time there most of my friends were moving up to secondary school whilst I should have been staying for one more year at primary school. For some reason I was allowed to move up a year early and made it my mission to prove that I was good enough to be in the older year group despite being the youngest person in my year at secondary school. I didn't enjoy school but was reasonably successful gaining all my exams at the end of my time there despite missing a reasonable amount of time playing tennis and doing things that I enjoyed. I managed to secure 11 GCSE's 9 being grade 'A' with the other two being grade 'B'. The most satisfying being in extended maths as my teacher was quoted as saying that he expected the whole group to fail because of my negative and disruptive attitude. In practice two people passed the exam – me and the girl who sat next to me!

I continued my education by moving to a sixth form college in Cambridge where again I was the youngest in my year group and still felt the need to prove myself. Again I managed to get through gaining my exam results at a level required to go to my university of choice (Grade B in Geography; B in Biology and A in Economics).

Sixth form became interrupted again by tennis but also by a back injury that saw me miss a reasonable chunk of time in my first year. On one of my sojourns out of college to play tennis in a study period I was short for time so I borrowed a friend's bike from the bike sheds to cycle to my tennis lesson. All was well until the tennis lesson over ran and I had to get back to college for registration. I decided it would be quicker to cycle on the pavements and not the busy roads so that is what I did. Unfortunately as I was haring down the pavement a car decided to pull out of a driveway. I was going too fast and unable to stop and hit the car and then veered off into the road only to hit another car and end up on the bonnet of the second car. I hit my head on the windscreen but although I was shaken I walked back to college carrying the decimated bike. When I returned to college the shock hit me and the tears flowed. I had a headache but thought nothing of it and continued the day. I went home and didn't tell John although I did tell Mum. I don't know why but I found it very hard to tell people when I was struggling. I went to college for the rest of the week but kept having to come out of lessons and then eventually ended up in accident and emergency a few days later with delayed shock and bruising to my head.

Time is a great healer although sometimes you wonder what effects a significant bump to the head may have on you. I sometimes wonder if the accident and the bang on the head could in some way have caused my present problems.

I have never wanted to be seen to be a failure. It is not something I want in my life. This desire not to fail has stayed with me throughout my life and has helped me in my battle against the voices and hallucinations that threaten to take over my life if given the chance. Sometimes it is not possible to overcome them and I feel a total failure as well as scared by the effects of the intrusions into my mind.

Chapter 4

The tennis journey of my life developed into something that would go on to shape my life in many ways – personal development, people I have met and who are part of my life, places I have travelled to and experienced and the contribution in varying ways to my health or lack of it.

My interest in tennis began aged 8 at primary school. A flyer was sent round the classrooms to see if anyone would be interested in signing up to a 'short tennis' course in a neighbouring village. Short tennis was a form of tennis played with a plastic racket and foam balls making it easier for young kids to play and enjoy. For some reason, still unknown to me, I took the flyer home and announced to my Mum that that is what I would like to do. I turned up at my first lesson quite early and saw a woman in the car park. I remember thinking 'oh no not a woman' when I really wanted the teacher to be a man – again no real reason for this thinking is clear to me to this day. Men held more importance to me in my young mind. I needed to impress to be accepted. Women did not have this effect on me so the motivation to do well was lessened. Little did I know how much that lady would shape my life in the years to follow. The session was great – I was fairly able and could play the game and continued to do so in the following weeks. The lady only took the first session and then it was a man, who turned out to be a fat, sweaty, unappealing lump.

Mini tennis progressed and I entered local tournaments the first of which I remember as I was runner up and I got a medal. I thought this was great, in my materialistic youth! After playing in a couple of these events I seem to remember being asked to play in a county practice and then in a regional and finally a national Mini tennis tournament. I lost in the quarter finals and was most put out as I seemed to believe in myself then in a way which is alien in my life today.

Eventually, aged 9, I made the transition from mini tennis to the game proper and somehow my path crossed with Sue the lady with whom I had started off in my very first mini tennis session. She was, at the time, the County Coach and I became involved in her groups and eventually her individual tutelage. Training became more frequent in both groups and individually and all school holidays were spent travelling around with a group of other kids playing tournaments. These tournaments were for players aged 10 and under to begin with but ages up to under 18's were at the same venues and a social learning was a large part of the experience mixing with other kids. You could spend days waiting for matches and then playing four in a row! At 10 and under I gained enough results so that when I was 11 years old I entered the National Championships that were to be held in Edinburgh, Scotland. Acceptances were done according to your results that you listed on your entry form and the top 32 players in the country in the under 12 age group were selected. I was very keen to go but expected nothing and when accepted was over the moon just to be there. We travelled up as a family, including Grandma, Sue was there as well as she had other players competing. I was envisaging being an also ran as I had drawn the supposed 4th best player in the event but went out in the cold windy Scottish elements and won through round after round eventually losing out in the semi finals and placing 4th overall – far exceeding the expectations of any one.

This relative success opened a few doors as it gave me some credibility with other players and I began to get accepted into more regional and national level competitions. By this stage I was having individual lessons with Sue on a regular basis a few times a week and seeing her most days in some tennis form or another.

I managed to get accepted for a National Winter series of events when I was 13 years old and the first one was in the north east of England in Darlington. I needed to play on Friday morning at 10am which meant I should have travelled up on Thursday. My problem was that I had a school field trip on the Thursday and had to travel early on Friday morning – leaving home at about 4 am to arrive ready to play. Not the best possible preparation, but surprising myself again I reached the semi finals which was, this time, my seeded expectation (although not my personal expectation as my self belief has never been a strong point – far away from my experiences aged 8!). Two more of these events took place and the third was in London. I loved being away for the weekends, and despite most other competitors phoning home

I never understood their need. I contacted no one and it felt a totally strange concept that others would want to. I was fairly self sufficient and felt that I could hold my own – maybe that was the cause of my next slip up? This was also the case in later years when I began travelling abroad. Little or no contact was made with home and no real understanding that people at home may be worried or interested in my progress. For the event in London myself and the other players were accommodated in a very nice hotel and in the evenings were largely left to our own devices. In the hotel on our floor there was a drinks machine that sold Bacardi and Gin, and the temptation was too great. Another player and I purchased some miniature bottles and shared them with others – hardly a heavy drinking session. The next day however someone in the hotel had complained and after much wrangling and explaining myself and the other girl who purchased the drink were sent home and banned from all National training and events and also any International duties which were on the cards. At this stage I had never played an International but was down to play in Austria in a couple of week's time which was now crossed out of the diary. Tennis life continued, training and competing locally when the News of the World newspaper published an article headed 'Tennis Aces Smashed' which detailed our 'off court booze sessions'. I found this quite amusing and the next day at school I became a cult hero for a few days as drinking was at that time considered cool as we were still under age.

Tennis continued with a break for wrist surgery to remove some extra bone that was getting in the way, and many ups and downs with Sue. We were very close but

I was finding that coming to an age when I wanted some independence the regime of doing 'as I say' was beginning to become difficult. To this day I regret not having made more of my own decisions regarding tennis and development (although I am not sure how well placed I would have been to make such decisions). How successful I may have been without Sue's knowledge and direction I do not know, but looking back I wish I was confident enough to be a collaborator rather than a listener and doer. This influenced me for a long time in later life where I felt ill equipped to make decisions, confidently, regarding myself, and wanted the security of guidance rather than ploughing my own furrow.

It was through this phase where I was first acquainted with T. He opened my eyes as far as tennis was concerned. He encouraged me to think and make my own decisions on court. I began to enjoy the game again and felt that whilst on court I had more autonomy, which as a teenager was welcome. I have never forgotten the input that T gave that day and the effect it has had on my life.

At the under 16 National Championships, in Bournemouth, another turning point was going to hit my tennis life and life in general. I was competing in the doubles final, which my partner and we went on to win. We were playing indoors because of rain. We knocked up and went to prepare to play. As I stood up I felt a sharp pain in my back. I didn't think much of it and thought it would pass with a couple of days rest. Afterwards it was sore but thought little about it. The following week was the 18 and Under Championships, I thought I would be fit to play. I tried but had to withdraw due to the injury. Little did I know that the injury would bug me for the rest of my life. It is all very well people offering you advice saying if you do not look after yourself you will have problems in the future – I could never see this and never entertained the thought that one day I would not be able to play tennis.

I played on and off with the injury through the summer.

I had started playing tennis with T as well as Sue and travelled to a 18 and under International event with T. I beat two good players to get to the last round of this big junior tournament and then had severe pain in my back and had to stop. I went to see a consultant who recommended bed rest for two weeks so I took two weeks off school and did nothing else. When I returned to normal life the back was no better. I had been prescribed Valium to help relax the muscles in my back (or so they said) and in my innocence I did not realise their addictive nature, however, I knew that they eased my physical pain and dulled my emotions.

This was to be my first experience of the 'numbness' that takes over your life on popping pills. I was to continue to use the rest of the Valium I had when I went back to school for my A levels as they were very good to have during stressful situations. I did not realise they were addictive but I did know they were enjoyable.

A couple of members of staff enquired as to my well being as they said I looked tired. As usual I gave them the typical 'I'm fine' reply.

I tried to play during the summer partly because I wanted to play and partly because I wanted to be with T. I had a turbulent summer of tensions what with my back and also because my parents were becoming very wary of my relationship with T which was probably quite obvious. It was during this week of my life where battling with injury and personal feelings, I knew I would be with T in a more personal relationship.

I came back too soon and played the summer Nationals but could not play up to my own expectations and hated every minute of it, despite my doggedness and determination to play – after all the game was a strong as any drug I have ever touched.

I returned to the National Championships again at the 18 and under age group which was held in Nottingham just weeks before I was due to start at Loughborough University just 15 minutes away. The event was played on hard courts which is not the best surface to play if you have a back problem.

I went and stayed there with T. although I told my Mum I was in Nottingham University accommodation. We stayed in a hotel nearby and every thing was going great guns. My back was fine, we had some freedom. Sue was there but no longer my owner, regarding tennis as I was spending more time with T and expectations of others were low as I had been off the scene for some time with injury. I started the week winning two comfortable rounds before playing the number 5 seed and again winning comfortably.

The quarter final was against an old adversary and I lost the first set easily feeling a bit stiff and sore from the day before. People were watching and I was losing confidence.

I may have been losing confidence but was far from losing the fight. I dug in and ran for a ball at 2-2 in the second set and suddenly my back was agony, I fell to the ground and I couldn't move or get off the court. People eventually helped me off the court. I could not play on. After a check over by the doctor at the tournament, he said he thought it may be a stress fracture so suggested I went home and got an x-ray.

My parents were called by T and they came to collect me. All my stuff was collected from our hotel and taken back to the tennis centre where I met my parents. After an x-ray it showed no bone damage and after some physiotherapy I was patched up and ready for University.

Following the summer, I had a further scan on my back which showed three degenerated discs at the base of my spine. This is incurable but the pain could hopefully be managed by injections to help relieve the pain around the surrounding joints, which were taking on the brunt of the strain that the damaged discs were supposedly causing. I have lost count of the number of injections I have had and consultants that I have trusted since 1990 when the problem first started.

Chapter 5

My education at Loughborough University, which was renowned for its sport, appeared to be ideal. I would be able to play tennis as much as I wanted to as well as trying to get through a degree which at the time was just something that had to be endured. Again, as at school, I was by far the youngest on the psychology major course that I had chosen. Many of the students had taken gap years or chose to study as mature students for a range of reasons. I chose psychology as it was only timetabled as four hours a week which seemed perfect to fit in with my tennis requirements!

I was 18 in the sports mad town of Loughborough. This was before any positive symptoms of my illness had occurred but was not without its stresses. The process of selecting a suitable University started with me trying to select a course to study. I scanned prospectuses of any University that had tennis courts or a sporty reputation as at the time tennis was my priority in life. Psychology at Loughborough was chosen partly because of the University's excellent sporting pedigree, but also because the advertised number of lecture hours a week was one of the lowest at four hours per week. Obviously extra research work was expected alongside this but in my mind and previous experience of academia (my A levels) this would not be too stressful and could be squeezed in amongst other commitments primarily tennis! Another reason for choosing a course with a low number of lecture hours was that my confidence was questionable and my fear of failing quite prevalent – surely even I could handle four hours a week and scrape by?

Weeks before the day arrived I was assigned a hall of residence just off the campus and preparations were made and all the paraphernalia was gathered for a move away from home. Some move away from home it turned out to be. Whilst plans were being made to move into the hall of residence T was also planning our move in together at a house in a nearby village. An end terrace was rented and as the day neared one of the most difficult days of my life grew nearer.

I moved into the hall of residence on the Sunday at about 2pm. Mum and John helped me to move in and unpack my stuff which seemed to be endless. They departed and twenty minutes after them leaving I myself was preparing to do the same. I called T and packed my stuff again. A quick explanation to the head of the residence that I wouldn't be staying and off I went to Kegworth with T to start the beginning of the next stage of my life. This was one of the most difficult things I had done as in my mind I was making a decision between T and my parents and I chose T. I loved my four parents but felt I had something special between T and myself that I couldn't walk away from. There was always the hope that one day Mum would accept this as part of me and the decision had to stand. I remember plenty of tears and emotional difficulties but also a huge sigh of relief that I was on my way forward.

The academic side of the course was interesting although I didn't make many friends as I left the psychology department as soon as lectures had finished either to play tennis or to go back to T who was spending his time in Kegworth doing I am not quite sure what!

My Mum and Dad both came to visit at Loughborough and I steered them away from the halls of residence with ludicrous excuses so they couldn't see my room. Eventually this became too much so I told them I didn't like the life in halls and had moved out to Kegworth with two other girls. It was then possible for visitors to visit and of course the other girls were always out, or away, or anywhere.

Studying continued and added pressure on myself with tennis commitments impinging on study time and a self induced pressure that I needed to achieve a 2:1 otherwise the whole escapade would have been a waste of time and effort (let alone stress).

In the summer vacation at the end of my first year I travelled to Belgium, Poland and Bulgaria with another player which is where my symptoms really took hold. By the time I returned to Loughborough I was really struggling.

At University this fear continued and grew with the onset of many of my symptoms coming to the surface. The fear of this and the need to live an undercover life lead to self imposed isolation being the safest option and the only way to cope. Lecture theatres became dangerous places to be with hundreds of unknown people packed in rows – no easy way out. All the time the pressure to achieve kept me going. At the same time it both made and destroyed me.

For the first year and a half T spent a large part of each week in Kegworth and Loughborough and was known at the university as he played tennis there with me and knew the other players. However, there is only so much waiting around for me that a man can do, especially without the creature comforts of his home rather than a damp student house.

As time progressed T spent less time in Kegworth and I would travel back and forth between Loughborough and T's home. I would spend the weekends with T and would train early on a Monday morning at a local tennis centre then drive to Loughborough for lectures and more tennis training. I felt as if I lived on the motorway. It became a hectic pattern but if I didn't lead a hectic life I would have had time to think and the risk that everything would fall apart. Tension held me together.

I became increasingly visited by voices and visual hallucinations. The voices would tell me that there was someone in the department that wanted to kill me and by reading my work that I handed in it would provide messages to the people as to where I was and some of the bad things that I must have done to be in such a position. It was a communication between us although I didn't know how to avoid it without totally jeopardising my coursework and work for University. I also had visual hallucinations of a woman with long dark hair dressed in black that carried a big axe with her. I couldn't understand why no one else was afraid of her and came to the conclusion that all of them must be in it together and I was the one who was in danger. I started to miss odd lectures and try to hide out in the library if I had to work.

Tennis again was my solace as on the tennis court I was alone and behind my glass wall to keep out such intrusions. Of course it didn't work but it was the closest I came to feeling in control of my situation whilst at Loughborough. Kegworth became scary as I had no defence there. I ostensibly lived alone with my own voices and visions to keep me company – some company.

Sleep was difficult as I did not know if I would wake up in the mornings and night times to this day are the worst times for me – the period immediately before I fall asleep everything appears to be hopeless and I cannot see a way of getting through the night. I wake up in the morning and the thought is *'how on earth am I going to get through the day'*

I did it. And I still do.

Chapter 6

Whilst at Loughborough University tennis was very much a drug for me and the more I could play the better, despite any injury. My course took up just four hours of lectures a week so with minimal input into my academic side of life, tennis took over.

Exercise became an obsession and being surrounded by other athletes it was more important than ever to be athletic myself (at least in image). With a minimal timetable it was time to take on the world stage of tennis and my quest for world ranking points ensued. I was not used to failing at anything so this was to be one of my biggest challenges so far.

The tennis was fantastic with a very professional approach to training and fitness work and some strong players to compete with. I didn't really socialise with them after practice however as I preferred to keep myself to myself and live my own life. Confidence was not a strong point and isolation felt as if it was a strong choice.

When you start out on the professional tennis ladder in the Ladies game the first rung on the ladder is to play $10,000 events. This seems like a lot of money but it shared between all the players. If you get into the main draw and lose first round you still get a small amount of money and then slightly more each round you win, the winner gets around £900. It is quite tough to get into the main draw and usually you are playing a qualifying competition with scores of others to try to make the first round. The tournaments then rise up from $25000 up to the really top ones which have mega prize money. From each tournament you play you get points depending on how far you get and it is these points that give you a ranking and from that ranking is determined which events you can get into.

In the first year at Loughborough I managed to get accepted into a $25,000 tournament in Ashkelon, Israel.

This was to be my first foothold on the professional tennis ladder and T and I duly headed off into the unknown in Israel.

It was a fantastic experience although I felt an enormous inferiority complex when I arrived feeling that I didn't really belong and that although playing well I was not up to the required standard. I played the girl who had won the event the year previous and lost closely which was respectable but a failure in my eyes which I was very disappointed with. It was as I say a first tentative step and I wasn't deterred despite my ambiguous feelings towards the outcomes.

Over the year the trips abroad continued, squeezing them in between tutorials and funded by T we travelled around Europe competing. In the meantime I would call my Mum every couple of weeks to say how things were going – still supposedly living in the halls of residence and studying hard – no knowledge of my tennis escapades were revealed at this time as I could not have funded them without T who was still persona non gratis with the parents. This was sad as I was desperate to share my adventures with them but it was not to be at this time.

Eventually I became caught out when another British player called them up to get hold of me as they wanted to travel abroad with me to another tournament in Israel that they knew I was going to. I then managed to tell my parents that I was travelling occasionally and funding it with prize money (which in reality was minimal).

As time and tennis travels continued, interspersed with life alone at university, I struggled silently with increased hallucinations and frightening experiences. It was the beginning of a long road.

Chapter 7

Israel was the first country I visited on this quest for a world ranking, subsequently I would visit the country on a further four occasions. In order to obtain world ranking computer points it was necessary to qualify for three point scoring tournaments (either qualifying for a $25,000 event or main draw for a $10,000 event). Israel on this occasion was a qualifying for a $25,000 event which because the prize money is higher the standard is stronger. In order to gain acceptance into an event it goes on your ranking. If you do not have a ranking it is difficult to get into events as you can only get points by actually being accepted. To start my quest I entered numerous events in Europe and waited for one without a full entry so I could compete as an unranked player.

The venue was a town called Ashkelon with a great tennis centre – as they all are in Israel, next to a golden beach. I was quite nervous but excited and spent most of my time at the tennis centre as all I wanted to do was play tennis. This was in my favour as I found out that during the first day a bomb had gone off on the beach and anyone on the beach at that time had to stay there until it had all been cleared up and therefore missed their matches in the tournament. For once I was not involved in the trauma at the event. I played my first match against the top seed and lost. I was frustrated and angry partly because I felt embarrassed at losing and the feeling that I was not good enough to be there came to the surface for the first time of many to come in future events.

I had some time before returning to England so T and myself, along with a couple of other players, travelled to Jerusalem for the day. The old town consisted of very narrow claustrophobic streets with very intense people bustling about. The Wailing Wall added to my fears of being in a fervent situation when I experienced for the first time a religious commitment by people that I could not relate to. I am not criticising peoples beliefs but my beliefs did not allow me to understand how driven these people were by something that I had no concept of – religion. I felt fear and could not get out of the place quick enough. It was a feeling of being trapped that I would experience a lot in later years. I vowed never to return to Jerusalem again, but against my better judgement on a later trip to Israel I repeated the trip only to have my fears confirmed.

I travelled to Israel alone on four later occasions and had memorable stays in Haifa and Jaffa. I loved to compete in the sun and the weather was always great in Israel. I was more competitive in the tennis and performed well there.

Haifa is in the north of Israel on the Mediterranean coast about seventy minutes drive from Ben Gurion Airport in Tel Aviv. I had arranged to meet a player who was arriving about an hour prior to me in Tel Aviv, and then we would share a taxi to Haifa together. When I arrived in Tel Aviv it was familiar as I had been there before. The arrivals hall was chaos and I could not see the player I had agreed to meet there. I could not handle all the people so decided to go and get a taxi alone. She would be ok – maybe she had gone already? In Tel Aviv Airport the taxis are organised so that the prices are fixed and the system is supposedly less corrupt. The queue was about an hour long and then a seventy minute drive until I was to arrive at the Israel Tennis Centre in Haifa. The other player was already there but accused me of leaving without her. She had seen me walking out of the arrivals hall and panicked and got a lift with an Israeli player, whom she knew was going to Haifa, and telephoned for a lift. I did not really care.

There were five British players in Haifa as it was a relatively weak event due to the frequent bombing of Israeli cities and towns. The bombing kept many people away, but for me served to make the experience more exciting. The tournament hotel was expensive, like most things in Israel at this time. It was also a taxi ride away each morning and evening which added to the cost. I managed to find a hostel where the five of us could stay in one room for the equivalent of US$5 per night payable in shekels. The room had three bunk beds and no room to put the notorious amount of luggage that tennis players travel with. We were to find out the next morning that the track we were to walk down to the tennis centre was also one that the local farmer used to walk his cows down to the fields! We therefore shared a short daily walk to the tennis accompanied by fifty Fresians.

As far as the tennis went, I was in the qualifying event along with eighty other players from all around the world. All eighty of us were fighting it out for four coveted spaces in the main draw where points and money were rewarded. In the qualifying event I won four matches, but lost in the final round so did not qualify. In the doubles I played with a German girl and qualified, we went on to lose in the quarter finals of the main draw to two Israeli girls. The Israeli girls were in the army, all girls had to do two years in the army, but these girls were allowed to train and play tennis. It was disconcerting as they were very manlike in both physique and attitude; and also put their rifles down at the side of the court during matches.

The trip to Jaffa was organised by the tournament. It was by bus from the event, and along with other players, we set off. It had become dangerous to travel by public transport as public buses were being targeted and bombed frequently. Not so many players came to Jaffa as some chose to leave because of the unrest. They moved on to play in more salubrious venues around the globe. The better you get, the better the choice as your improved ranking helps you to gain acceptance into a wider ranger of tournaments.

I had decided by this point that I did not want to stay with other players at the expensive official hotel. The rest of the Brits had gone home and I felt that I must not be extravagant and spend T's money freely. I did not want people to think I was only there to buy computer points but wanted to feel I was there on merit.

I moved out of the official hotel and with my considerable amount of luggage into a small hostel en route to the Israel Tennis Centre in Jaffa. I shared a room with eleven others, none of whom I knew. I slept in a top bunk along with all my rackets and possessions. By this stage I was in a phase where I did not want to eat so I lived on Mentos fruit sweets (the tournament doubled the price during the week because of the demand) and one piece of pitta bread per day. Again, I did not want people to think I was living off T so I lived on minimum provisions. I took lots of exercise and no food – the only way to feel good these days.

As far as the tennis went I was in qualifying with 80 other players who were aiming for 4 places in the main draw where points and money become available. In the qualifying event I won through five rounds of matches, playing girls from Croatia, Israel, Serbia and 2 Australians to earn a place in the main draw and was very happy and relaxed – nothing to lose. Having reached the main draw panic set in, with the immediate thought that I am not good enough and that I did not deserve my place there. I seemed to have a fear of losing and a fear of being judged as being not good enough and as a result played very inhibited tennis to lose.

Israel at this time was a little unstable and the night I went to Planet Hollywood with a couple of friends to pass the evening, a major bomb blast took place down the road at the Hard Rock Café. Many people were killed and the next day the street was covered in flickering candles and tea lights to remember the less fortunate – a memory that will forever be etched in my mind. On the back of this bomb blast many players headed for home but for me this made the trip more exciting.

The events in Israel are held at big venues often with men's events running alongside the women's tournament. I met a Chinese player in the men's event who was very laid back and funny – I would later cross paths with him and his team mates in Indonesia.

When it came time for me to leave Israel my flight was quite early and I was travelling with El Al the Israeli carrier. To get through departure when travelling El Al takes about 3 hours. Crazy I know but a fact. You are quizzed by three separate officials on details of all your travel during your stay. They need to know exactly where you have been, where did you stay, details of all the matches and interestingly 'Why did you lose?' Good question!!!! This is normal in Israel and so did not bother me too much except that to get to the airport for the flight I had to leave the hostel at 5am. My problem was that the hostel was locked until 7am for security reasons. The night before I needed to leave I found a large ground floor window and made sure it was unlocked. The next morning at 4.30am I left my eleven sleeping companions and made my escape through the window to the street with my luggage.

❖ ❖ ❖

During the summer vacation from University, I planned a trip to Belgium, Poland and Bulgaria. I was not going to travel alone and travelled with one other British girl. We travelled to Belgium and stayed with a great family in Rebecq. It was the first time that I had played in an open qualifying tournament and was quite taken aback when I saw the draw sheet with 128 players listed. In truth I thought that I had no chance! I lost 1st round qualifying, I was right – no chance! The second week in

Koksijde, a beautiful seaside resort was similar with an early defeat but this time we stayed in free accommodation in a disused hospital near the tennis centre. All the players stayed here but we had the sense to nick some of the loo rolls so we had a supply before everyone ran out!!

In planning the trip I had decided to take travellers cheques. For the second week of the trip in Belgium I needed money but only had large denominations of cheques so did not want to change them into large amounts of Belgian Francs, especially as all the accommodation was free of charge. This meant, however, that my friend and I had no money to live on. We got fruit from the local grocery shop and stayed in bed all morning so that we didn't have to eat until the evening! We then bought a chicken from a local shop and devoured it between us on the beach! I was finding it hard to spend time 24 hours a day every day with tennis players and craved my own space which I found being able to run on the beach. This was the beginning of a long lasting importance of running alone. This escapism was becoming more important for me as all I seemed to want to do was to be alone. My confidence in being surrounded by tennis players (all of whom in my own mind were better than me) was at an all time low. I dreaded the matches and felt embarrassed at being there.

The next stop was Poland. We had a nights sleep in Brussels airport, we flew to Berlin where T joined us and hired a car to drive across the Polish border to Gryfino – a tiny village with a big tennis centre. Everything was so cheap that you could not spend your money even if you tried so we had plenty of catching up to do after a weeks scrimping and saving in Belgium. I did not fully realise it at the time but this was to be the first time that I heard voices abusing me and directing me. I was very scared and could not concentrate on the tennis but that was fairly insignificant. Tennis suddenly didn't matter – why was I suddenly surrounded by this voice and people? When I came off the court I was very upset and walked up the stairs into the club house. At this point I vowed never to come back to Gryfino again. That is something else I never managed to live up to as one year on I was back again!

I felt different, I felt hunted. I never thought 'Why me' or 'What is happening', as I felt completely consumed by the fear and was unable to compare myself to others. I felt very exposed, scared and unsure of what was reality. It all seemed real to me so I had no question at the time that it was real or not. If people say to you that someone will kill you, I could not see a reason to disbelieve them. Looking back now I can view this more objectively, but when it happens in the current day I feel the same fear I felt in Gryfino. I felt totally isolated despite all the invasions into my head but I felt so threatened there was no way I could tell anyone. The fear permeated right through me and I was sure everyone in the world could see it in me. This for me was just the beginning.

After Gryfino we drove back to Berlin to fly to Sofia. I have never been so relieved to leave a country and I was hoping to leave behind my experiences.

Flying to Sofia in Bulgaria with Balkan Airways was not the greatest experience but we arrived safe and sound.

We hailed a Skoda to carry three of us plus tennis bags to Bourgas – a three hour drive. All the bags were somehow strapped to the roof and we squeezed in. The drive was along some quite hilly windy roads. Our driver, to save on fuel, would switch off the ignition on every down hill stretch and then switch on again as we hurtled into the bends of the road. We were overtaken by another Skoda at one stage of the journey, but this one was special as the boot was open and a live bear was chained to the car standing up in the boot! I was ready for anything after that! We arrived in Bourgas and proceeded to cross a railway line at top speed. The bumping over the tracks at such a rate caused the roof rack to cave into the car through the roof. The driver was most disgruntled and seemed to think that it was our fault. Eventually we arrived and all was well.

Again everything was cheap in this town on the edge of the Black Sea. Players and coaches were given vouchers to purchase their meals in the Hotel Bourgas Park restaurant. The food usually pizza, was so cheap that we could not spend all the money the tournament provided for meals. Our solution to this, being the athletes we were, was to spend all the excess vouchers on litres of rough, cheap, red Bulgarian wine. T did his best to keep up with the supply, but even with our help we ended up bringing many bottles home with us as generous gifts for family and friends.

To get to the tennis courts from the hotel it was a short walk through the 'park'. The park was a scruffy, scrubby area of land with a few trees and bushes. When walking through the park on the way to the tennis one day, I had the shock of a Bulgarian tramp leaping out from one of the bushes and exposing all he had got. I was stunned and left very quickly and ran to the courts. Was that another person who was watching me.

The tennis was pretty average once again. I felt more exposed on the court and in danger of people wanting to kill me as that is what I was being told by the voice that had taken over my mind. The tennis court used to be my haven but now it seemed like a display arena for anyone who wanted to threaten me. Understandably the results were poor and that added to my unease on the court as my confidence by this time was none existent. I couldn't talk to anyone about it as I was in danger and felt once again that I was wasting everyone's time and money and couldn't justify my existence.

Varna was the next stop on our tour of never to be missed gems on the Black Sea. We arrived at Bourgas airport (a small airport only servicing internal connections) and presented ourselves, passports and tickets for the flight. All three of us had purchased our tickets at the same time, same place in England before the trip. On checking in we were told by a very unattractive employee of Balkan Airlines that only two of us had valid tickets and the other person would not be able to travel. We refused to move and stuck together. After 40 minutes of haggling in broken English, which was increasing in volume, another official came along and solved the problem thus allowing all of us to travel. The mode of travel was a very rickety propeller plane for an hour long flight to Varna. As well as being lucky to get on the flight I think we were luckier to arrive safely.

Golden Sands was the resort name with red clay courts distributed around between hotels and beautiful pine trees. Music and jewellery were dirt cheap from stalls along the sea front. The Bulgarians however were not hospitable like the Belgians and I did not feel safe. Despite this, again the following year I returned to a place I disliked.

One thing that I did enjoy throughout these summer tournaments on the clay courts, that you do not get in England, was the time that I could spend practising. All I wanted to do was be on court (matches scared me as after a couple of terrible weeks in big qualifying draws my confidence was fairly minimal) but practice became my escape. I loved to practice despite the fact that I was suffering dreadful pains in my back.

I thought that if I pushed myself hard enough I could override the pain and the voice. This was a desperate attempt to cope with the voice and hallucinations of people I would see, especially a lady carrying an axe who seemed to be following me about. Also by practicing hard I felt I could lose weight which was again high on my list of priorities. My body was something I wanted to destroy as it was only there as a source of mental and physical pain.

The way in which I saw myself was often through the values given to me by others – my interpretations of the values lead me to low levels of self esteem and confidence. The 'real self' that I hoped for was a long way from the 'ideal self' that I seek.

As a competitive tennis player every day I was presenting myself to other people by being out on the tennis court alone. As I never thought that was good enough it became more important that I at least looked good. The desire to be better (perfectionism?!), the desire to please others, the search for acceptance, the need for control, low self esteem and low self worth were the feelings that went on to fuel what some may see as a destructive behaviour pattern. Despite feeling alone in these emotions it is the case that professional or amateur athletes can be 16 times more prone to eating disorders than those in other sectors in society. The need to constantly improve myself meant that I was never happy with how I was and improvements could always be made.

I had a tennis playing friend who I travelled stayed with for three weeks during tournaments. She used to be 'big' but transformed herself into a very slim (in my mind) athlete who was also successful on the tennis court. Everybody was saying how good she now looked and I thought how great it would be to look like her. Six months later she died from an illness related to her eating disorder – the thing that scared me though was that I still wanted to be like her – did she have the ultimate control?

As a tennis player sport and body image was (is?) very important to me. Especially at the time when I was at University when every spare minute of the day was spent on court, running, swimming or any other calorie burning activity that was on offer. I only did this when I was alone but the return for the efforts were to feel 'high' from the exercise and to feel hungry from eating as little as possible to get through the day. This keeps me in control.

Food and eating became a controlling force for me, and in the face of the voice and hallucinations it was something that I was still able to manipulate. I have the power to eat or not to eat (at least I like to think that is the case). By not eating and creating a hungry feeling I feel in control. Eating was minimal and at many tournaments my nourishment would come from Werthers Original sweets or Polo mints just to get some sugar and to make the hunger tolerable when playing. If I was on my own I would sometimes treat myself to a bowl of plain rice but not always. Alongside this self deprivation I used to travel around the various countries that I visited by the cheapest transport possible – bus, train, or even hitching a lift on one occasion. I would stay in cheap hostels, as I did in Israel, sometimes sharing a room with as many as 12 people whom I had never met before. I did not want people to think that I was living off T's money and wasting it without thought. Self deprivation was the way to justify myself – I don't know who to. These were times when I felt I had more control and I think they were some of the best times I have ever had.

Eating in front of other people for me is something I find remarkably difficult. It is difficult for me to be seen as indulging myself or treating myself. I feel greedy or weak if people can see me in meal time situations – I feel out of control. Eating is my thing that is very private and not open to others. It is a self inflicted situation which can often result in secrets or secretive behaviour. Secrets are becoming harder to keep, especially as people in my head know exactly what I am doing and watch every move. I live my life with a running commentary going on inside me with the voice (that incidentally I believe to be outside of me) commenting on my every action. I wanted to let people into my world slowly, to understand where I am at, but also I need people to leave me alone to be where I want to be and to where it is safe to be.

Merely by talking about where I am now is difficult for me. Admitting that I have a weakness in myself is hard. It is like inviting people in to watch what I am eating which is a big thing for me, as feeling watched is something that I struggle with day in and day out. It is to me a stupid as taking a drug in public. I do not really want help or others to know. I know that if I was on my own I would have no problems. I would eat enough in my own way to survive and would be happy doing it.

* * *

Thailand was the first destination that I travelled to alone.

The excitement started when I booked my flight from the cheapest offer in the News of the World – Benz Travel. The flight was with Aeroflot (Russian Airlines) to Bangkok via Moscow.

From Heathrow I was upgraded to Business Class for the first stage of the journey. Although this was not the same as British Airways Business Class, it was better than Aeroflot Economy as I was to find out on the next stage of my flight. After a 4 hour delay in Moscow we boarded the plane again. I was the only female passenger and more and more people kept boarding. In the end for take off there were men sitting on the floor in the aisles. It got better. When we eventually took off the men were obviously ready for the journey, as they proceeded to get out of their hand baggage, roast chickens and apples. The chickens were torn apart and shared around with bones and apple cores just left on the floor. The Vodka came next and the smelly Russian sitting next to me did his best to get me to partake. As the black and white Russian movie did not grip me I decided on the sleeping pill option – what I am not aware of cannot harm me!! The next I knew I was woken up by a Russian air hostess and the plane was on the ground and empty. We had made an unscheduled stop in Abu Dhabi and everyone had to disembark. As I had taken a couple of sleeping pills I could hardly keep my eyes open I was scared stiff of missing the plane when it eventually took off again. Fortunately I made it and 22 hours after my take off in London, which seemed an age ago, I arrived in Bangkok.

I rescued my bags and found a taxi to take me to the tennis centre at a university in Bangkok. I had about 3 hours to get there before sign in for the tournament closed – I began to relax. I was unprepared for the traffic in Bangkok which was nose to tail and each for themselves – relaxation went out the window! Having been travelling for nearly two hours I was getting worried, the taxi driver obviously had no idea where we were going. Eventually I saw a person walking down the street with a tennis racket so I leaned out and asked for the courts. By some miracle they were the courts that I was searching for and I arrived from half way around the world with ten minutes to spare!!

It was blistering heat as April was the hot season so I decided to try and practice a little before competing the next day. I found a Thai girl to practice with but on walking to the court I trod on a drain cover that was not fitted properly so my foot ended up caked in sewage from the drain. I practised, lost about half a stone in fluids, and returned to the hotel. It was a great modern hotel across the road from the tennis. To get there the choice was air conditioned mini bus, which took about 40 minutes to get around the one way system and across the Bangkok traffic, or I could risk dodging the traffic and risking my life crossing the road on foot. This became the initial puzzle each day as I headed out to the tennis.

The tennis was OK but pretty uneventful. My back continued to hurt, in fact more than before, so decided that after I had lost in the first week I would go and see Steve, my brother, who lived in the city. I called him and got a bus to where I thought a good place for a tourist to start would be. I had all day before meeting Steve and wanted to see some of the sights. I asked the bus driver to let me know where the stop I wanted was. After 90 minutes he motioned for me to get off – we were exactly where we had started from but on the other side of the street. I decided to walk, and walk, and walk! I saw many sights including a brief trip around the Grand Palace but I had to leave my passport at the entrance in exchange for a skirt and some rubber shoes to cover up my legs and feet which were taboo in such places. After the Grand Palace I was walking through a fairly touristy area when a Thai man came up to me and started walking alongside me. I thought he was

going to try to sell something or a tour trip but when
he found out I was English all he asked was whether
I knew Margaret Thatcher! This opened a conversation
and then we both went our own way. This reassured me
that Thai people are very gentle and well meaning
and Bangkok is one of the places that I have felt most
at ease and safe in. I walked to Steve's apartment and
had a great evening which included my first trip on a
tuk-tuk. These were like mopeds with a couple of chairs
stuck on the back using one was both exhilarating and
nerve wracking at the same time - all part of the Bangkok
experience though!

Steve came back to the tennis with me for the second
week and couldn't believe that people were actually
playing tennis in such humid and hot conditions. I had
to play a girl that I had played before in Brunei which
was good as I won, but a shame as I had come all that
way to play someone I had already competed against.
The next round was the end of the tennis for me so
I hit the markets instead! The Ramkaenghaeng Road
where I was staying had a great market with clothes
stalls and fake goods all over the place. I stocked up but
also discovered mango sticky rice which was a glutinous
sticky mess that tasted heavenly. I stretched my boundaries
and allowed myself to eat this as it tasted so good and the
alternatives were often unrecognizable!

As I had less than a week left I called Aeroflot to confirm
my flight bookings home. I was silenced when they said
that I could have a seat from Moscow to London but
they could not fly me to Moscow as they had over
booked the flight. I thought that as I had a fixed ticket

my seat was safe, but apparently with Aeroflot there is no such thing as safe! They suggested I went to the airport and stayed there to try for a standby flight that may take a week to come available. I rang England and the British Embassy who advised that I go to the airport on my departure day and try to book another flight with another airline. I did this and trawled all the airline offices until at last the British Embassy arranged for a BA flight back to London. The catch was that to get the affordable price I had to pay in Bangkok. I tried this but my Visa card was rejected as I was over the limit. A few more frantic phone calls later to T and the ticket was booked from London but at an extortionate rate. I eventually got in a queue to check in. When I reached the counter I needed £30 in Thai currency for airport tax – I had none! I grovelled to the man behind me in the queue and he paid for me – I could not thank him enough, and boarded my plane home. It was quite an adventure for my first trip alone but one of my favourites none the less.

Travelling alone held no fears for me, in fact it was quite liberating. The hallucinations were still with me but as I ws alone I didn't have to worry about others finding out about me. It was easier to isolate than to risk being uncovered which would put me in more danger. I was happy to take risks travelling alone as I had nothing to lose. I didn't really care about myself so what would it matter is something happened to me. I wasn't particularly close to my parents at that time and the only person I felt close to was T but he was still not openly in my life as my parents did not yet know about our relationship. My life seemed like a tangle of secrets and stresses but that was normal for me.

Chapter 8

I was to return to Thailand a couple of years later with J, a renowned player from Surrey. We met in Bangkok as she was travelling from Japan where she had been competing in the World Student Games. I had persuaded her to come to Thailand as it was such a great place the last time I had been there. She met me at the airport and said she hated it – such a dirty smelly city. Within hours of exploring she had changed her tune. The people were fantastic and the culture so diverse you cannot fail to be mesmerized. We travelled Bangkok mainly on foot but we also used the local transport mode of the tuk tuk. The traffic was crazy with motor bikes, scooters, mopeds and conventional cars alongside the tuk tuk all jostling for position, changing lanes, creating new lanes, and all this to the hooting of horns. As the day progressed the tuk tuk drivers would become increasingly intoxicated, and the rides became more exciting. In the evening the street came alive with markets, selling bargain fake clothes, watches, jewellery and music. In fact anything you really want can be obtained as long as it was a copy. The process of acquiring any purchases demanded an extended friendly conversation with the seller, and a protracted bartering system with the seller tapping prices into a cheap calculator. This appealed to the two of us as we both had very limited finances and we entered into the bartering experience of Bangkok market shopping whole heartedly.

We had a night in Bangkok staying with Steve in a room almost on top of the railway. He only had one bed free so J slept there whilst I took my place on the cold tiled floor by the door. Steve equipped me with a baseball bat in case anyone tried to get in through the dodgy door, and also a large can of cockroach spray to keep the little buggers at bay! Early the next morning we decided to go to Pattaya for a couple of days before going to Khon Kaen for the first tournament. Steve assured us that Khon Kaen was only a couple of hours away so we could have 2 whole days in Pattaya before catching the bus in Bangkok to the north east. Pattaya was amazing – full of middle aged sleazy German men and their rented out Thai girls. We checked in to the Flipper Lodge, very salubrious, and as we had had a heavy night the previous night we slept on the roof around the deserted pool until about 6pm. When we woke up it was to discover that the pool was the local pick up joint with very strange couples doing what they had come to do!! This became a daily routine for us after nights out in sleazy Pattaya South Beach entertaining with our superb singing in the karaoke bars!

On returning late one night to Bangkok Steve announced that Khon Kaen was a bit further away than he thought and it would probably take 12 hours. This meant leaving at 4am to get there for sign in at 5pm the next day. The phone lines were poor in Khon Kaen as it was quite a remote place. There was no way we could ring ahead and tell them we were on our way so that we could be signed into the tournament by phone. The bus journey was horrendous with some of the worst driving ever displayed through the monsoon rains on single carriageway roads. Overturned lorries and trucks littered the sides of the roads as testament to the nations driving ability. We arrived, once again cutting it fine as to getting there on time but we did. The next horror was that matches started at 6am in order to be finished each day by noon when the rains came. A one eyed driver called Boo, who was a student at Khon Kaen University transported J and I around the town. In return we promised to fulfil his wish of having a picture of the Queen. Khon Kaen was otherwise pretty uneventful despite a couple of efforts in the local karaoke.

The karaoke took place in the hotel 'night club' located in the basement. J and I had indulged our limited skills before on karaoke audiences in various venues on our travels, so we decided to do the same again in Khon Kaen to pass the evening. The night club consisted of arm chairs around low tables with a karaoke 'menu' on the table. The place seemed quite empty at 11pm and we started to plan our attack and scan the menu. We put in our chosen numbers at the bar and waited to be called. No one else seemed to want to sing. There was music on and we sat waiting for our moment. When the microphone was delivered to us we staggered up to the stage at the front of the night club to face what we thought was a fairly empty venue – we were wrong. Little did we realise that the other high backed comfy armchairs were all full and that the occupants had been singing their karaoke choices sitting down. Not us! Now we were on the stage we had to perform and we strangled a few songs to rapturous applause from the Thai audience that appreciated the effort. The singing was awful but they loved English visitors as they got very few in their area. The Thai people are extremely polite and we tested this with our performances. This politeness encouraged us (along with a few drinks) so we danced and sang for them until 4am. It was a great success for us with the exception of my forward roll off the edge of the stage to crucify my back.

After the excitement in Khon Kaen we had to travel back to Bangkok and stay for one more week. We had booked tickets on the air conditioned bus as the temperatures were so hot and the journey was twelve hours long. After thirty minutes into the trip the air conditioning packed up and we baked in our seats for the next eleven and a half hours. It was a relief when our travels by bus were over.

The rains continued and the tennis was average but a good time was had by all and Thailand remains one of my favourite places visited to date.

* * *

My visit to Croatia happened to coincide with the war that was raging in that part of the world at the time. On this occasion I didn't travel alone but went with another British player.

We arrived in Zagreb and went to the official hotel. It was a building with a UN flag outside and the first 5 floors were for refugees from the war. Our room was OK but then I decided to go to lunch on my own. It was unrecognisable sloppy stuff! I didn't eat much but what I did eat certainly had an effect as my stomach reacted violently for the rest of the day! The next day we changed accommodation to some student housing a walk away from the tennis centre.

The tennis was looking good as I was practising well as usual and enjoying myself. However when it came to match day nerves set in and I lost in a very frustrating match to a girl from Serbia who looked like my mother. I was so stressed in my first match that after the first game I broke a racket in frustration and then again after losing the first set. I had two left for the next week. It wasn't something I could explain to my colleague who was watching in amazement as I hit the self destruct button as early as game one of the match. I felt so inadequate on the court and having my colleague watch I felt even more pressurised as I was spending my life at this time feeling watched and followed. The voice was having a free run of my life as I was disintegrating with ease just as he said I would – he was right again. I felt he was so intrusive he was really getting into my mind. I heard him as a man shouting at me but I couldn't see him, he seemed to be everywhere where I went but I have no idea what he looks like. I think he is about 40 years old – not a young voice but not old either. Very aggressive, sometimes as if he had been drinking, but always in control never showing any weakness.

Zagreb was a great city with a big central square where everyone hung out in the evening. Most people were soldiers of some kind mixed with a few young locals. There were a couple of pizza joints in the square so that is where we spent most evenings. Zagreb also boasted a free (we didn't pay!) tram service. To pass time we tried every route around the city on the trams and began to see areas of the city that had been affected by fighting and the war. The fact that the people of Croatia were largely soldiers gave me more concern as there were plenty of people who had the means to kill me if they so wished. I couldn't avoid them and this added to my anguish during my trip to Croatia. I had no desire to compete on the tennis court although as usual practice and hard work pushing my body physically was a method used to try to banish the mental pain.

The second week was on a small island called Brač in a resort called Supetar. The tournament arranged flights for the players to get to the venue for the second week. This was not straight forward as the flight path would have to go out to sea and then back in to the coastal town of Split, as it was not safe to fly directly over Croatia. From Split it would be an hour boat ride to the island. The flight was ok but we were the only people not in combat clothes or working for the UN which was frightening for me. The boat ride was great as the sea was calm and the weather fantastic. The island was beautiful but once again was full of soldiers as it was used as a venue for their rest periods.

The tennis was questionable on my part, especially as I trashed both of my remaining rackets in practice so played my match with a broken frame. My mind was struggling at this time but I had not told anyone about that sort of thing so I just played tennis until I hit self destruct where my rackets took the brunt of it all.

The rest of the week I spent sunbathing on the rocks near a quiet cove with beautiful clear warm water. The only distraction was being able to hear bombs on the mainland and see the occasional grey battleship drift past.

At the end of the week we had to make the return trek to Zagreb to catch a flight to London. As it was quite a time consuming trek we had to travel to Zagreb the day before our flight out. We intended on sleeping in the airport at Zagreb but were advised not to. A Croatian girl came to our rescue saying that we could stay, along with a Belgian girl, at her Grandmother's house about 30 minutes from Zagreb out in the countryside. Her uncle collected us in his 2CV and we chugged through some of the most beautiful landscapes which seemed a world away from what had become the norm of soldiers everywhere. I had a fleeting thought that maybe I would experience peace here? This was not the case though as I always had the stress of returning to Zagreb the next day and then back to my life in England. The Grandmother was very welcoming and was also completely self sufficient with chickens in the garden with vegetables growing alongside. Dinner was predictably chicken with beetroot juice to drink, rounded of with a glass of thick sour creamy milk stuff that unfortunately or possibly fortunately, I dropped on the floor. The flight the next day was uneventful flying via Vienna which seemed like a different planet, unfortunately.

Croatia is one of the most beautiful countries that I have visited and will always remain etched in my memory for that – especially the kindness and hospitality of the Grandmother in the country. However as usual the positives were far outweighed by my fear of the voice and what it said, the pain in my back and hatred of myself during the time away.

✻   ✻   ✻

Portugal is a country that I only visited once on my tennis travels and that was enough. It started out Ok and I arrived in Lisbon at 7pm local time. I found out that to get to my destination of Elvas it was best to get a bus at 7am the next morning. This was fine so I found somewhere to stay near to the bus station and took the four hour bus journey the next day. I planned to return to the same hostel on my way home as I would have to travel back to Lisbon the day before my flight home. I loved the travel it was a time to be alone and to try to wander aimlessly to shake off any followers. The fewer people who knew where I was exactly the better as I did not want to encourage followers who may want to kill me.

I took the bus from the very unremarkable village of Elvas on the Spanish border back to where I thought the central terminal was in Lisbon. As it happened I was told to leave the bus at another stopping point in Lisbon. I had all my bags and a scruffy street map so I started to walk to where I believed the hostel was. After 2 hours in the heat of the day I made it. In the afternoon I decided to go and visit the castle in Lisbon which is situated at the top of a hill with beautiful gardens surrounding the winding path. I got there and admired the view before walking back down the hill to the town again. The path was not empty and seemed safe enough when all of a sudden a man in a leopard skin loin cloth jumped out from the bushes with a knife and grabbed me. I was in a panic but policemen suddenly appeared and dragged the bloke off. I was left standing there a bit shocked and surprised. That seemed to be it though so I continued on my way. That was Lisbon's claim to fame and is how I will always remember Portugal! Was this what Arthur (the voice) looked like?

✳   ✳   ✳

Seville was one of my most enjoyable weeks in Europe. I arrived and went to the tennis which was 30 minutes from the city. The official hotel was expensive but there was no where else nearby so I checked in. The next day I lost to an American girl and again was struggling with my back so did not play doubles and did not want to spend my time at the tennis. My opponent was staying in Seville city so I went back with her to the hostel that she was staying at for $4 per night in the city centre. There were no rooms left but the lady who owned the hostel allowed me to sleep on the roof for the same rate. This is what I did. Seville was hot during the day and very lively at night where I met up with other people who were backpackers travelling around Europe. I heard some great stories and met some really interesting people. This reiterated my belief that I should be staying off the beaten track in other countries that I visited after Seville.

✳   ✳   ✳

Germany was a country that I visited several times whilst playing for a club in Bremen. In the German league it is common for teams to financially support players from abroad. I was asked to go to play for

Bremen as their number one player and as usual was very nervous about the whole thing. We played teams from the region around Bremen, and were fairly successful. The team were very German and insisted on showing me all their latest material goods as well as telling me how much money they had spent on each item. The tennis was not a really high standard but very competitive and was played in the evenings in the winter. All the members of the tennis club came to watch each fixture. It was a big event for the club. This was quite daunting as I was the foreigner who was being paid to play and was expected to win. Most of the matches I did win. As a result I was then rewarded with drink after drink from the club members. This was so different to the attitudes held at the tennis clubs that I have been a member of in England where any outsider is just that and is not made to feel welcome in the slightest. In the summer the matches were played on the red clay courts which were great. I really enjoyed the surface but it was not my best especially as I travelled back to England during the week to play on grass courts – the complete opposite. Again the standard was not too hot and we won our league and progressed through to play in a different area. For the away matches we were provided with cars from the local dealer and again were treated like royalty throughout. I really enjoyed the experience and felt very flattered that they paid me to do this when I would have been quite happy to play for the fun of it. I no longer keep in contact with the club and guess that most of the other team members will probably have normal day jobs by now – just like me!

❖ ❖ ❖

I travelled with T into an area of the world which neither of us had experienced before. We went to some of the former Soviet States.

Our first trip was to Lithuania only. We arrived in Riga Airport, which is in Latvia but closer to our final destination of Siauliai in Lithuania. It was dark in the evening and very cold. The airport left something to be desired but luckily we did not have to hang around there for long. Unlike most tournaments this one provided transport from the airport to the tennis centre venue. We were met by a Lithuanian driver and a lady who worked for the embassy and could speak both English and Lithuanian. The van had a long crack from top to bottom of the windscreen and certainly no heater. The conversation was a little tricky but we managed to establish that although it was very cold it never snows in Lithuania. We thought it would be a straight forward sixty minute drive. It turned out to be an eventful two hour trek! The roads were empty as fuel was at a premium and it was not long before a police car appeared out of the darkness on the unlit road. We were waved down. Our driver went to the police car and came back ghostly white after about twenty minutes saying to the translator in mad Russian that we needed to give the police money to continue otherwise they would not allow us to drive on!! On offering a US$5 bill the driver nearly took my hand off and rushed back to the police. They were over the moon – they were only earn $5 a month if they were lucky!!

We arrived at the hotel and had to go through a rigorous stamping of forms before being allowed to go to our room. On every floor there was a hotel guard just sitting by the lift but it was difficult to establish their exact role. It was another throw back from the old Soviet Russian way of life. It was so cold we both went straight to bed in all the clothes that we had with us to be ready for the next day.

Looking out the hotel window the next morning in daylight brought the sight of two foot deep snow drifts! So much for the drivers words that it never snows in Lithuania!

The tennis centre was a mini bus ride away – quite uneventful this time although still using the bus with the broken windscreen. The centre was fairly new I think as the paint on the radiators (cold) was still wet! The limited electrical supply meant that only 3 of the 4 courts could be lit at one time so this was done on a rotational system in which courts were lit for an hour and then not for the next hour etc! There was a small coffee bar in which to order hot tea with huge amounts of sugar in, but this was the only place with a semblance of warmth. The tea was a bargain. The exchange rate was 200L to the pound. The cup of tea cost 5L. This appealed to my desire not to spend much money on my tennis trips and we drank enough tea to last a lifetime.

We met a Swiss girl travelling with her mother so decided to have dinner in the hotel with them each evening. The dining room was pitch black with a small tea light on each table so it was impossible to see what you were presented with at the table. The food was unimaginable. It was a risk trying it. The only good thing was that the nightly bottle of champagne shared by T and Mrs Switzerland only cost the equivalent of about 80 pence. And so the week progressed. The dining room had a large dance floor in the centre of the gloomy room upon which the local prostitutes gathered and tried to attract business. I did not know who their clients would be because the only people in the hotel were female tennis players and their coaches. I cannot imagine who would visit this depressing place. It was so dark and cold in the dining room / dance hall that the prostitutes all wore fur coats and long winter boots. Not a centimetre of flesh was on show. If they did have a client I could not imagine anyone taking off their clothes, they would freeze to death.

We were to discover though that the ladies of the night were quite proactive in their pursuit of trade. It was 2am on the first evening and T and I were in our two narrow hard single beds with one thin blanket each. In order to combat the cold we slept in shirts, sweatshirts and anoraks. There was a sudden knock at the door. T called out to enquire who it was and the lady said she was selling cigarettes and could she come in. T declined but she, or another compatriot, tried the same trick every night, often several times to get access to the bedroom for a bit of business.

In a search for nourishment we hit the streets of Siauliai. There were odd people selling cabbages which did not really tempt us too strongly but then we found the queue for bread. After queuing up for half an hour we realised that the locals were buying one or two tiny bread rolls each at around 4p a piece. Although embarrassed we bought rather more without trying to wipe out the days supply for the locals. This became a daily routine.

Tennis results that week were better quarter final singles and semi final doubles.

When it came to leaving the same mini bus appeared to transfer us back to Riga. The snow was thick and the roads quite dodgy but the same old driver just grinned at us and a Finnish girl and her coach who was also with us for the journey back. We stayed in the same lane that had been created by the other limited traffic until we came to a slower car in front. Our mad Russian driver decided to go for it and overtake. We spun round and round and somehow managed to avoid the other car and only just avoided the deep ditch at the side of the road – the mad Russian just grinned, righted the bus and continued! We survived.

The following November I decided to go back to play the same tournament again, this time following it up with a week in Jurmala, Latvia. Siauliai had not changed much – the hotel was the same with guards on each floor and limited electricity and hot water from 5 – 6pm each day only. The town had developed a little with a few more items on sale and prices had picked up marginally but there would be no known reason for people to visit without a mad cap mission like a tennis tournament in the middle of winter! Our mad Russian driver appeared again unbelievably with the same bus with the same cracked windscreen – no excitement this time though. There must be something about this part of the world as

I usually get good results on the court. This time last 8 singles and doubles

Jurmala is by the coast in Latvia fairly close to the capital, Riga. The beach is a fantastic expanse of pale sand with trees and big old run down wooden houses along the land side. At the weekends people seem to come out of the woodwork and even in November the beach life was prolific. Only one old lady ventured into the icy Baltic and I got the impression that she was the mad Latvian who did this every weekend all year round!

Jurmala was more developed and stylish than Siauliai and it gave the impression that at one time it would have been a place for wealthy families to have a holiday home. Now, it is little more than a ghost town for the most part.

Whereas I did not find much to like about Siauliai apart from the generosity and hospitality of the locals, Jurmala was a different prospect. The wide roads, trees and beach were very relaxing, and I loved the isolation of walking along the beach in freezing temperatures, looking out at the lonely Baltic Sea on a daily basis. Only at the week end was the loneliness shattered as the locals emerged and took to the beach. It was great to see the enjoyment and happiness of the people in temperatures of minus 10 degrees. This was their social Mecca, for there was nothing else in Jurmala. One of my memories is of a beautiful flower stall on the street side – buckets of vibrant flowers against the grey of everyday life in Latvia. These images still stay in my mind.

The tennis centre in Jurmala was a little more up to date and welcoming with the bonus of lights on all five courts all day. I competed much better but lost in the semi final to the number 3 seed 4/6 6/7. Played with more desire and felt good about it. This may sound as though this should be normal but as I have said before I have never been a performer and found the practice court more enjoyable for my best tennis.

I went home on Baltic Airlines from the shed of an airport in Riga, the Latvian capital. The plane was quite large but there were only about 50 passengers bound for London. The flight was uneventful until landing. The touch down was smooth and the pilot put on the brakes and all the unoccupied seats collapsed and folded forward. Nothing dangerous just a little disconcerting! I left Siauliai, Jurmala and Balkan Airlines never to return.

Chapter 9

Throughout my travels and time in between in England I was working to raise some money as a tennis coach. I had taken my first two levels of coaching exam and had a place coaching at an indoor tennis centre. I loved coaching as it meant I could stay physically active and could run about all day burning calories and pushing myself as well as my clients to their maximum. I enjoyed the variety of seeing different people each hour of the day as it meant that none of them were with me long enough for me to let my guard drop. It was very important that people had no idea of the danger I was in and the risk that that posed or me. I felt I could keep myself safe for the one hour lesson and then had a few minutes to compose myself before the next client. This is a pattern that would follow in some of my counselling work in later life. Tennis travels were still high on my priority list though as I began to taste freedom and enjoyed taking risks with the way that I travelled and the people who I chose to socialise with when abroad. I would book a flight to the country I was visiting and then I would take it from there when I arrived at my country of destination. No one would be informed of my whereabouts when I was away. What did it matter?

✻ ✻ ✻

Indonesia was a trip to remember. I did not know it at the outset but it was to be the last part of my competitive tennis journey. I travelled alone to Jakarta which was a long 13 hour flight. As usual I had not booked any accommodation or onward travel arrangements – it would all just happen somehow and somewhere. When I arrived in Jakarta at approx 8pm I was waiting for my bags reading a map that I had just picked up trying to decide where to stay for the night before heading off to Bandung the following day. Whilst waiting, a middle aged couple came up to me and started talking. They said they were from Holland and had seen me reading Russian on the plane (that I was trying to learn at the time). I wondered what on earth they wanted and why had they noticed me on the plane? This tapped into my being watched and followed but for some reason I chatted to them waiting for our baggage. They said they had come to visit their daughter who lived in Java somewhere and they could speak Indonesian. I told them I was going to try to find somewhere to stay on Jalan Jaksa (a travellers street). They decided they would do the same so we could travel together. This seemed strange to me and the voice was taunting me that they were out to get me. One of my big problems though is not being able to say no. The Dutch couple seemed quite adamant and organizing so I went along with it. Not with any specific fear just the usual from the voice. As I have said before I didn't really place any value on my safety as I had nothing worth losing. It seemed reasonable and a better idea than travelling alone at night in a foreign city. We grabbed a Bajaj (three wheel tuk tuk type vehicle) and headed for Jalan Jaksa. On the way we got held up in an enormous hold up. The fly over express way had collapsed onto the road we were trying to travel along. There were cars and bodies everywhere and rubble and dust amongst rescue workers. At this time, about 11pm, it started to rain. When it rains in Indonesia it never drizzles but absolutely tips it down. We were squashed onto this open bajaj with our luggage precariously balanced. After a few hours we made it across Jakarta via a different route away from the carnage. Jalan Jaksa was a tiny street hardly wider than the bajaj but the Dutch guy jumped out and found two rooms for us. It was about 2am when I finally made it to my room having agreed to meet for breakfast at 7.30am the next day.

My room was OK. There was no lock on the door so I piled up my bags against the door and headed into the bathroom. It was a square concrete room about 4 foot square with nothing but a bucket of dirty water in the middle on the floor – I gave it a miss. The room itself had a small window but with no glass in it and the bed had no sheets. The strangest thing though was that the room had a telephone next to the bed – seemed rather out of place with the minimalist theme of the room. I slept OK and went down the next day to find the Dutch couple eating toast. I told them where I was hoping to travel to and they suggested that instead of getting the train I could go by a shared taxi. They took me to the taxi place and I waited for about 30 minutes until there were 11 people who wanted to go to Bandung where I was headed for. I bid farewell to the couple who wandered off in search of their daughter, and still can't quite understand why they adopted me for my first day in Jakarta.

The taxi bus took 5 hours to get to Bandung through beautiful countryside with rice fields and tea plantations. We stopped for half an hour to buy some bananas. These were mini bananas that were sold in a bunch of about twenty. As I only wanted a few I gave the rest to local children who thought their luck had come. A couple of hours later I was in Bandung. It seemed a different world from Jakarta. Again the journey with strangers enhanced the feeling of danger for me and I felt it was getting nearer to the time when someone, whoever it was meant to be, would kill me. Part of me wished they would hurry up as the tension was unbearable and all this time I was unable to tell anyone about it. The voices threatened me if I told and for some reason which I still cannot understand today the voice commands power over all others. He still does.

The hotel for the tennis was quite posh and I managed to find two Australian girls that I could share a room with to keep the cost down. It was raining again so there was no practice so I went to McDonalds for a coke. The locals appeared to be quite intrigued as to why a white person would be visiting Bandung and many came to talk to me! Eventually I even managed to persuade my room mates to come out with me although they seemed to be scared of their own shadows in this different environment. Why?

The tennis was okay. It was played on courts that were like very old tarmac school courts in England. They were not flat so many players seemed to come off with twisted ankles or similar injuries. I eventually lost to a Chinese girl who went on to win the tournament and I can't remember the doubles – it must have been riveting!

The evenings were spent in the hotel Karaoke bar singing and dancing the hours away. This seems to be a strange behaviour that comes over me when I venture to the Far East!! I was away from any one or anything familiar so stood up in front of the locals to share my not very promising musical ability. Part of the reason was to test myself to see if I could still hold my nerve against Arthur, my voice.

The following week the tournament was back in Jakarta. Every other player in the event had a plane ticket to fly back but I decided to take the train. I arrived at the station and a man came to ask where I was travelling to. When I told him Jakarta he took my bags and vanished. Oh shit I thought I would never see those again! The train pulled into the station and I boarded the economy carriage and the luggage mysteriously appeared! Well worth a few quid for the stress value alone! The economy carriage had no seats and open windows but I had decided to take this option as I wanted to see what it was like. The cost of a first class ticket was only 80 pence more – maybe worth it for a seat as the journey took nearly 5 hours through breath taking green scenery with rivers and waterfalls interspersing the tea plantations and rice fields.

When I arrived in Jakarta I had no idea where I was heading for apart from the name and address of the tennis centre. I grabbed a cab and showed the address and we set off. After about an hour we arrived at a shopping centre and he said I had to get out as we had arrived. No tennis courts in sight but I had to get out! I wandered around and asked a couple of people where the tennis was. The couple said they would take me so again finding myself unable to say no and not being particularly worried about my welfare I got in their car with them and it was only after we had set off I thought what on earth am I doing getting into a strange car with two complete strangers? They tried to be helpful as we turned up to a solitary tennis court and they asked me who I was going to play with – a slight communication error. I again showed them the address of the tennis centre and we returned to the shopping centre. What is going on I thought – they showed me downstairs though and the tennis centre entrance was underground the shopping centre – made it at last!! The centre was beautiful with trees and a swimming pool. I shared a room with a German girl and had a great week with some success in the tennis despite struggling with a knackered back again.

Whilst in Jakarta the Davis Cup was being held between Indonesia and China. As I had met the Chinese number 1 in Israel we had arranged to meet at the Davis Cup. I arrived without a ticket and said at the gate that I had come to see P (the Chinese guy). The men at the gate were suddenly very helpful and took me straight into the men's changing rooms!! I rushed back out asking if I could get into the stands. They took me to the section for Indonesian VIP's. I was the only white person there and also the only person rooting for China! P saw me in the stands and when his match started he walked to the back of the court and started talking to me!! I thought

I was going to be lynched by the Indonesian crowds! After the match instead of sitting with his team mates on the court P came up to the stands and sat with me. When his team mate Xia lost the first two sets P suggested that we went for some lunch. His chauffeur driven limo arrived and drove us to a food court. After about an hour and a half we wandered back to the tennis to see that Xia was still playing. We went back into the stands to see the last game of his five set victory. I left as I thought P may have been strung up by the Chinese team for being so unsupportive – he did not seem bothered in the slightest. Having been champion of South East Asia for the past 4 years he was somewhat of a superstar and did not feel the need to put himself out for others – typical man!!

I visited the markets of Jakarta with an Australian girl from the tournament and we bought fake everything until we had almost no money left. So little money that when we went back to the airport to leave for our next destination (mine being London) we sat and sang songs collecting money to buy a drink with!! Very desperate and totally deranged after three weeks in Indonesia!!

I boarded the flight which was quite empty but we had to stop in Kuala Lumpur for an hour. I felt really tired and my back was killing me so I didn't bother to get off in KL but stayed asleep. I remember thinking I will never make the flight home as my back was killing me and Arthur was making it clear that the plane would crash and that would finally be the end of me – he would have won. The next thing I remember is the stewardess on the plane trying to move me to the business class section of the plane as I was having some sort of panic attack, although I didn't know what it was at the time, I vaguely remember being injected with something and then the next thing I remember was waking up in a hospital in Madras with a dead body being wheeled out next to me. I was terrified.

Apparently I had gone into some sort of rigid position. I could not move anything and looked as though I was a dummy. I was awake but not able to speak.

The people on the plane had recognised that I was not very well and without my really knowing they diverted the plane to Madras. BA had to dump hundreds of gallons of fuel in order to land at Madras airport. I was rushed to a hospital where I would be safe. They did not know what the matter was with me and my memory of the whole escapade is very sketchy.

I spent a few days in Madras hospital and had a few more of these 'attacks' but cannot recall much else apart from being fed rank curry for each meal which I refused to eat. Eventually on the last day a porter brought me a banana which was the only thing that was not curry spiced so I ate it with relish. I had spoken to T whilst in the hospital and he was trying to sort things out to get me home. All sorts of tests were done on me during my few days in the hospital, but nothing emerged. The pain in my back was so bad that it was difficult to bear.

I received a phone call and thought it may be from T but when I made it to the phone it was from the reporter from a newspaper in England asking questions about my illness. I was even more confused and cannot recall how the conversation went or ended. I could not understand why they should be the least bit interested in my problems. After a few days the doctor who treated me was flying back to London with his family and he had arranged with T that he would look after me on the flight back to London. I flew back with them. I was wheeled on to the plane in a wheel chair as I was so weak but had four seats to stretch out on and slept most of the way home. I was fed some rice and a lot of fruit juice which made me feel more human again and by the time we reached Heathrow I was able to walk off the plane to be greeted by the press!! Why?? I appeared on the front page of all the major newspapers. It must have been a quiet news day. It was fame for fifteen minutes, definitely not by choice.

It turned out that the lady who had helped me on the plane was a nurse. On her return she contacted all the papers and I had appeared on all the front pages of the national press. My photo and heading such as 'tennis star in plane diversion'. I was greeted by T and my Mum and J and did not really know how or who knew what about where I had been or what I had been doing. It was to be a long round of investigations after the event that eventually would lead to uncovering Arthur but not for some time yet.

That was Indonesia and my last tennis trip abroad as I slipped into retirement!! Probably a good job as my trips were becoming more precarious as they went on.

Chapter 10

After graduating from Loughborough tennis was my life. However injuries were never far away and a troublesome back injury eventually ended up with surgery. After endless physiotherapy throughout my university time to keep me on the tennis court as much as possible the inevitable happened. A scan showed that the sciatic nerve was not moving smoothly through its canal of bone and therefore a procedure was carried out to widen the canal. The surgery was reasonably successful for about twelve weeks when all the pain returned. I thought I had recovered well from the op and was back playing tennis seven weeks after the surgery – this in hindsight was far too soon and it was therefore not too surprising that my body objected – this was to become the story of my life. I continued to play tennis as much as possible but two years later after my fateful trip to Indonesia I underwent surgery again.

Again the process was to be similar to the first one but at a different level in my spine. This time I came round from the anaesthetic and had an attack similar to the one that I suffered on the plane returning from Indonesia. I was scared stiff and kept suffering from these attacks throughout my recovery. What happened was that all my muscles would go into spasm contorting my body and giving me painful cramps. I would not be able to speak properly as my tongue was also contorted and for some time after the spasms had worn off I would speak with a stutter until I had completely relaxed again. The process was very scary as I did not know the cause and had no real way of controlling them. The surgeon that had done the operation had left the country to lecture in the USA so was not on hand for my recovery which was less than satisfying. The staff nurses in the hospital believed that I was having these 'attacks' as I didn't want to go home – I don't think this can be further from the truth. I kept the curtains closed in my hospital room and the lights switched off. If I could get away with it I would have the door shut too so the bloody nurses who I thought hated me would not intrude. I was frightened but not for the reasons that the nurses thought. I saw another neurologist who followed up my treatment on leaving the hospital (the surgery was unsuccessful) and he referred me to a psychiatrist as he felt the attacks were more psychologically rather than physically based.

This was difficult for me to hear as I did not want anyone to know about the voice that I heard and the people that I saw. I felt like he had seen my weakness and that threatened me. At this time people around me were against this view that the attacks were psychological although I knew that I was dealing with voices and hallucinations which I was too afraid to acknowledge. I was referred to Dr L who always wore very nice suits and was quite personable but I did not really like him. I sat talking to him for an hour on our first appointment and told him nothing. Eventually he referred me to a clinical psychologist called Jennifer who I subsequently saw on a weekly basis for several weeks talking mainly about my eating and exercise habits, which was all that I admitted to having difficulties with. These sessions with Jennifer were difficult as I knew that I had something to hide and that I couldn't tell anyone for fear that something may happen to me. The longer it went on the harder it became and the more I felt threatened.

After a period of time and several of these 'attacks' later I was admitted into the Wellington Hospital in London for a week (which ended up as 6 weeks) ostensibly for depression and to observe me. I was prescribed meds which made me drowsy and also Dr L wanted me to undergo a course of electroconvulsive therapy (ECT). I didn't know much about ECT then but just said OK as I didn't really care. I explained to T and to my Mum that was what was prescribed but cannot really recall much more about it as one side effect of the ECT is to lose your short term memory which I did. I was coming round from the anaesthetic not knowing who T was or where I was and simple names or my home phone number etc. I think had plenty of visitors but cannot recollect any but I know we went out of the hospital for walks in the nearby Regents Park which was cold but a welcome break from the ward. Sometimes the nurses took me to the coffee shop on the corner for an espresso which woke me out of my daze for a short spell. There were no groups or structured therapy (according to my recollection) although I regularly saw my psychologist and the consultant psychiatrist. On days of my ECT though I was not allowed out of the ward and had to rest for this period of time. This carried on for four weeks twice a week having ECT until Christmas Eve when I was allowed to leave and went home, still on a high level of medication. T had arranged a holiday for me and on Boxing Day I went on holiday with T and two friends to South Africa but have no recollection of any of it at all, even when I see photographs of it I do not have any recognition.

Anyway I survived. I was back at work – some minor miracle although I still didn't think there was anything wrong with me – or was not prepared to admit it to myself and definitely not to anyone else. I was working three days a week for Marylebone Cricket Club at the famed Lord's Cricket Ground in North London. Coincidentally the ground is overlooked by the hospital that I had just been discharged from. I do not know if anyone from work knew I had been in there and I certainly didn't think anyone knew the reason for my stay – that was still a mystery to me as again I thought I was OK (or liked to convince myself of this).

I kept regular weekly outpatient appointments at the hospital with a clinical psychologist to whom I told nothing, and also regular appointments with the consultant psychiatrist whom I divulged even less. The psychologist focussed a lot on my eating behaviour or lack of eating and low weight which I thought was nothing to do with her as it had never caused me a problem. It felt like they were trying to find a problem to label me with something. She made regular appointments for me with a dietician who kept prescribing me with sweet high energy drinks which became meal replacements for me rather than in between meal top ups. I felt resentment at someone trying to control me and began to feel like the walls were closing in. People were taking an interest in my private life which I had always considered to be very private and not something to be shared. In my upbringing I think I had been encouraged to cope and to get on with things and as I was fairly competent at life no one had ever questioned this process. Now professionals were trying to find a way in and I felt very threatened. The voice became more prominent talking about how much at risk I would be if I spoke and the fatal consequences of such admissions.

Eventually it came to the middle of February when the psychologist decided I had turned a corner (from where to where baffled me) and that she was going to reduce one of the drugs I was taking called Thioridazine. Thioridazine had been prescribed as an anti depressant for me and this reduction was an unusual move as the medication changes came largely from the consultant and not the psychologist. I was not about to complain. I had my own agenda.

I had been feeling low for a long time, voices were talking to me telling me to self harm – I had begun to cut my arms in the hospital with a bathroom glass that I smashed on the floor and kept some of the shards for this purpose. When people ask about cutting and want to know why all I can liken it to is smoking – You know it is not good for you but the feeling that you experience once blood starts to flow is like a release and a high that you experience in very few other situations. It is like the reward for the 'bad' behaviour and is very addictive. I was hallucinating seeing people and generally had had enough. I started to formulate my plan. I thought I could save up enough tablets to make an attempt at my life – I didn't have anything to lose (that is how I felt at the time despite T being there for me as usual and my family were a bit more in the background at this stage). Depression makes me very selfish and makes me focus on me more – my own black world. I decided to go for the overdose option and just needed a time when I could do it. Then I came off the Thioridazine which brought me out of my sedation somewhat and gave me the energy to put my plan into action. I think it would have been too much if I was still on all my medication but a cloud had lifted and I had energy on which to act. I waited until T went out one afternoon to a friends wedding reception, to which I was not invited – we still were not accepted as a couple at this stage. It was 2pm on March 14 1998. It was to be my last day – I was ready to act or at least thought I was.

I took the remainder of the bottle of thioridazine and waited. Nothing happened and I began to get impatient and worried. I decided to make a phone call to a good friend just to say goodbye and to leave a message for T. I suddenly realised I hadn't left a note which I felt was rude!! My priorities were a bit jumbled at the time but I still remember the time clearly – it was moving in slow motion. I asked my friend to explain to T what I had done. The next thing I knew there was a knock on the door which I got up to answer – I was a bit unsteady on my feet but made it down the stairs to the front door of our first floor flat. I got the shock of my life when I opened the door and there was an ambulance crew there for me. I think they were just as shocked that I answered

LUCY ADAMSON

the door as if nothing had been going on. Again I still
didn't think I had done anything wrong, but why were
the pills not taking effect? Had I not taken enough? The
ambulance crew came up stairs and then T arrived as
well. We were rushed to the local accident and emergency
department in a nearby hospital. At this stage I remember
very little despite knowing I had my stomach pumped
immediately and was admitted to a ward. I think at this
stage I must have slept for a long time as the sedative
effect of the overdose took effect even though my stomach
had been emptied. My next recollection was of waking
up in hospital and not knowing where I was but just
feeling this crushing disappointment that I was still
alive. How could I fail at my last action? – the story of
my life – failure, or so it seemed.

I do not know how long I spent in the hospital but
when I left I was readmitted to the private psychiatric
ward for another four weeks and more ECT. From this
point again my memory is sketchy – probably the effects
of the ECT.

Chapter 11

During this period of time Jennifer the clinical psychologist whom I had been seeing went back to America – her home country. I was referred on at this stage to another therapist called Annie. Annie was completely different and I felt comfortable with her straight away, however I was still carrying a secret of the voices and hallucinations that I was experiencing. I was still under the umbrella of the psychiatrist Dr L and felt that I had been seeing him for a fair amount of time and even if I had the courage to talk about my hallucinations it would be difficult to suddenly mention it so far down the line. I kept quiet. I had weekly sessions with Annie before work in London. She was a respite hour at the beginning of the day and I looked forward to seeing her despite still maintaining my secret. I was deteriorating under the stress of keeping quiet. I used to travel to Annie on the train into London in the rush hour. In one of my more desperate moments I took a razor blade, which I had handily hidden in my purse, and started to cut my wrists on the train. The train was full of people but I continued as once you start to cut yourself the relief is huge. It wasn't an attempt at my life but merely a need to get relief (and the voice was telling me to do it which reinforced my feelings). When I got to Annie's I kept my hands in my pockets of my coat so that she couldn't see but during the hour I inadvertently took one of my hands out and she saw the blood running down my hands. Luckily there was also a doctor working in the same building and he cleaned up the wounds and bandaged them up. I returned to work after my session and continued as usual. Again not one person asked about my bandaged wrists. Not that I wanted them to do so - I couldn't care less. It says something about people though that someone can sit in a rush hour train hacking away and then arrive at work all bandaged up and people turn a blind eye not knowing what to say. I think people were scared of me when in reality I was petrified myself. Annie recommended that I had an inpatient stay at the Priory hospital where she also worked and she communicated with Dr L and referred me on to a Dr R. Dr R was also a psychiatrist and I had an appointment with him to see if he felt it was a right move for me to be admitted as an inpatient. It was this interview with Dr R which proved to be something of a turning point. I had no intention of telling him about the voices etc but half way through the session which I was already quite emotional in he asked me point blank if I heard voices. I felt he could see inside me and I was totally vulnerable. The voice was shouting at me not to tell but for some reason Dr R seemed to be on my side and I nodded my head. I could not say the words but when he asked me the question I tried my hardest to communicate to him that I was hearing voices. I did not tell him at this stage that I was also seeing things as this seemed a step too far. Dr R explained to T what was going on which was a huge relief and I was admitted as an inpatient the following day at the Priory Hospital in London. I cannot remember much more about this conversation except that it was a monumental step forward for me in giving me a chance against my demons. I believe Dr R also told my parents about the nature of my illness but again the details are elusive to me.

I stayed as an inpatient for about five to six weeks and it was my third hospitalisation in as many years - this was to be a pattern to be continued for the next two years as well. The time in the Priory was spent in therapy groups all day every day which were to be endured although I am sure some helped with self confidence which was at an all time low and I still had huge difficulties talking about what was going on in my private world. Everyone was supportive and Annie also came to visit regularly as she was working in another part of the hospital at the time which was a great support as well. I started on some different medication and was taking Stelazine which kind of helped to dampen down the severity of the voices a little but the voice has never gone away.

I continued to see Annie and Dr R as an outpatient and over time the Stelazine was not working as efficiently as it would have been liked so I went through phases of trying some more modern meds in the form of Olanzapine and Risperadol. Neither of them cracked my problem and antidepressants were added to the cocktail to try to lift my moods. When I suffer from the voice and hallucinations my mood darkens – this is not really a great thing as the darker my mood the more the hallucinations take hold so it is a vicious circle. After about 10 months of this tinkering with levels Dr R suggested that I try a drug called Clozaril. This was explained to me to be a fairly successful drug in controlling symptoms such as mine but the drawback was that it had to be done under supervision and regular weekly blood tests at first to monitor possible effects on my white blood cells. In order to have this monitoring it would be impractical to use DR R and my private medical care so I needed to be referred to an NHS psychiatrist.

My NHS psychiatrist agreed to put me on Clozaril but again for the early days I would have to be an inpatient to be monitored. The NHS psychiatric ward was a far cry from the hotel like Priory and was an experience I will never forget. On arrival I was assessed by a doctor that I did not know and he asked questions such as what day is it? Which I could manage!, then it got harder as I got more flustered as he asked why I was there and I responded that I heard voices. He asked if anyone had told me I had schizophrenia which I replied 'no'. He followed this with a question as to 'who is the leader of the opposition party?' which, now in a total spin, I replied 'Ronald Reagan!' I guess that rounded off that assessment for the day! I went back to the room I had been allocated only to find another lady in my bed and as I was so scared of people following me and wanting to kill me I was scared stiff by someone so blatantly within my personal space. This was nothing unusual in the ward. I started on the Clozaril and had the blood tests but ended up staying for about a month in the ward. Part of the reason for this was that they were convinced I had an eating disorder which I denied and they thought I was taking my medication and then making myself sick so I was watched every morning and night to check I was not doing this. To get back at them one evening I took a bottle of Procyclidine, (a medication that I was taking to try to reduce the unwanted side effects from the other drugs that I was taking at he same time) that I happened to have in my handbag and which I was taking before admission to the ward. I took all of it and then waited. When my behaviour became strange (taking a bottle of Procyclidine gives the same effects as having a bad acid attack) and I was careering around the ward in and out of peoples rooms, I told them what I had done. It wasn't a dangerous overdose as it happened but it lead to me being up all night and most of the next day in a surreal state hallucinating more than ever.

Facing my public (T and Mum) the next day was much harder than deciding to take the pills. To explain to them how I didn't want to live or be with them anymore was a real test. It is not because I don't want to be with them it is because I can't bear to be with me. I seemed to care less about leaving them, with me dead, than I did about hurting their feelings by telling them about my attempt. It is difficult to describe but when I have made attempts at my life they have been totally selfish and motivated by my feelings about me and how I cannot bear to be with myself any more. These feelings still occur today on occasions when the voice is too scary or controlling. He often says just 'end it all, you know you want to do it', which on many occasions I do but somehow do not have the strength to fail again.

During my stay in the ward we had weekly 'conferences' with all the staff who were involved in my case and a general update on how things were going. It was at one of these events that I asked, perturbed by my initial assessments mention of schizophrenia, what my diagnosis was. It was then when I was told that it was paranoid schizophrenia 'of course' – as if I already knew but wasn't accepting it. I survived my final few days in the ward and then left with great relief. I was blood tested every week in order to get my meds and during this period of time my brother, Steve, and his fiancé, Ding, were getting married in Bangkok but because of these blood tests I was not allowed by the doctors to travel as I would miss the vital blood tests. This is something that I greatly regret.

Whilst being monitored for the Clozaril I received daily visitations from the Community Mental Health Team (CMHT). This visit was dreaded as I had nothing to say to them and had no respect for these people that invited themselves to my house because I supposedly needed them. I was very paranoid at the time and having strange people coming to the house was quite threatening. I took to carrying a baseball bat with me everywhere just in case I was attacked which was what I was expecting at any moment. I did not have the identity of who was going to do the attacking so I had to keep my guard up at all times. I even went back to work at the local tennis centre as an admin person in the County Office for tennis. I took my baseball bat into work with me and not once was I confronted as to why I carried it at all times – even if I just went up the corridor to get a coffee. Another prime example of the caring British nature!!

I was also having trouble with the television set in that I thought that the people on the TV know who I am and what I am thinking. If I was to watch a detective or crime programme I would be convinced that the people in the programme knew that I knew 'who did it'. I would get stressed because I didn't know but felt that I would be threatened if I didn't communicate with them to let them know this. This is still the case today to the extent that I only watch minimal TV if at all possible to remove this threat. Some public figures that were on the TV were particularly menacing including Ken Livingstone (the then Mayor for London), Michael Howard (the then leader of the Conservative Party), Mo Mowlem (a politician who has fortunately died now so I do not have her stalking me any more), and also Desmond Tutu. If any of these characters saw me whilst they were on TV I felt they could control me and manipulate me to put me into danger. I had to be very clever and cunning to avoid this confrontation.

The Clozaril was prescribed every week after a blood test and it made me very sleepy without really controlling my symptoms to any great extent. After a period of about 12 months I went to New York to stay with my brother and his wife who I felt very close to. I was as happy as I had been in a while. Suddenly I started fainting for no obvious reason. The fainting was to become a recurrent issue for me for the next few years with the combination of the drugs, the fear of Arthur, the fear of being followed and being the subject of a hit squad etc.

Chapter 12

After my first stay in the Priory I was still being treated for severe back pain and underwent the third spinal operation by a different neurosurgeon he specialised in nerve damage. He had identified a disc that was unusually bulging out to the side and pressurising a nerve thus giving me serious pain in my right leg all of the time. This had been the cause of the problem all the time but had not been identified by the previous consultants. He operated and all was well. I followed up the surgery with a more structured rehab although as usual Arthur (my voice) had input into this and the rehab stopped prematurely. The voice made me very wary of the physio that I was working with and I felt that he would end up killing me if he got to know me too well. I was afraid to be alone with him and felt suffocated during the 2 hour sessions that I spent with him. Also in order to recover I was given a rigorous physical rehab programme and the voice was adamant that I should not do it as it was going to risk my health if I continued.

Gradually I was suffering with more leg pain so I returned to the surgeon. He had moved on so I saw another specialist who passed me on to another who suggested I had injections. I did it but got relief for about two months after he had inserted a camera into my spine and treated the damaged areas with an anaesthetic type fluid. When this wore off the pain returned. Boring I have been here before.

Later on I was to discover that the nerve that had been under pressure causing the pain had been pressurised for too long and had become damaged. Even though there was no longer any actual pressure on the nerve it was still responding as if there was. All in all it was as if there was just too much to cope with so I just fainted in a state of total overload. This however was a complete unconscious decision and not a thought that went through my head 'oh I have too much on I will hit the deck'. It was not until many occasions later that I began to see the pattern of overload and realised I had to be careful when things were building up. Of course Arthur (the voice) loved the whole procedure talking about failure and attention seeking and then that maybe the next time that I fainted maybe I wouldn't wake up again and would just die. My NHS doctor agreed that the Clozaril was not working for me and I got back in contact with Dr R. I was admitted again into the Priory ostensibly just for a week to alter my meds again.

On arrival at the Priory I was allocated a room and left to unpack. All my belongings were searched and deemed harmless enough and then I just had to wait to be assessed by a doctor. I eventually saw a doctor and he decided that I should be in an observation room behind the nurse's station because of my 'vulnerable state of mind'. I was on ten minute watch supposedly for my own safety. I had a different idea. I was petrified in a new place (even though I had been an inpatient before) and Arthur, my voice, was being particularly intrusive and abusive saying that the nurses were plotting to kill me and I was not safe. I decided it would be a better option to finish myself off but I knew I only had a maximum window of ten minutes in between nurses coming to check on me.

I found in my belongings some metal coat hangers which I bent round and wrapped around my neck. The plan was to hang myself in the wardrobe, a method which may seem to have its design faults, but in the moment it seemed a good idea. I was in the process of trying to hang myself up in the cupboard when the nurse came in. I had failed again. Even more scared Dr R was called and he decided that I needed a 24 hour watch for my safety and supposedly to help me feel more secure. Within half an hour Gloria came to be my special nurse who would be with me. She sat in my room and tried to calm me down which I didn't really want and I ignored her. I was started on new medication called Amisulpride which was an anti psychotic aimed to help reduce the intrusiveness of my hallucinations. I had a nurse in my room all through the night and also if I wanted to use the bathroom in the corridor I had to leave the door open. Half of me craved privacy whilst the other half felt relieved that there was someone there for me.

Dr R came the next day and had a longer chat during which he told me (in the presence of Gloria) that he wanted to increase the Amisulpride and also wanted Gloria to note down my weight and what I had to eat and drink. I was really pissed off. What has my weight and eating got to do with all this? Looking back I now know that I was only so perturbed because he had foiled one of my plans – if they want to control me I will control my eating. The Amisulpride dose increased sharply over the next couple of days and affected me by making me quite drowsy and 'fuzzy'. Everything seemed to slow down including my speech and I felt I was walking like a zombie. I was lying on my bed all day without speaking to Gloria. I had extra Haloperidol if I felt bad at any stage which was fairly frequently in the first few days. I had asked not to have visitors for the first week so was able to just be semi comatose in my room with the ever present Gloria.

The following morning I was quite sick and was finding all my muscles stiff and difficult to move. I couldn't sit up on my own and couldn't see clearly. Speech as well was laboured with my mouth not seeming to work properly. When Dr R came round he prescribed a drug to help with the side effects and suggested I carried on with the Amisulpride. The next day was no better and I had a visit from T. I felt so embarrassed and ashamed at my condition but could not really speak to T. He read from the newspaper to me which was great and in the end I was glad he had come. He knew nothing of my hanging attempt and I wasn't about to divulge – it meant nothing to me and my current condition was more imminently concerning. Following his visit T complained to the staff that my condition was unacceptable. They said only Dr R could change things. T then made a call to Dr R about the level of medication. Dr R decided the levels of Amisulpride were too high for me to cope with so stopped it completely to give my body a chance to recover. It worked and a couple of days later I was able to walk and talk normally again. Arthur also came back with a vengeance.

I started again on the Amisulpride at a low level and stuck at that for the next week. I was still on 24 hour watch and didn't venture out of my room all day – I was too scared and didn't' know who might be out there. Gloria was becoming more tolerable but wanted to watch TV which scared me as I felt like it was talking to me and could see inside my mind, ultimately controlling my behaviour and thoughts – again I was out of control. Annie visited me in hospital and managed to smuggle her guinea pigs in to cheer me up – which they did –it was the highlight of my stay!!

I was still finding it difficult to keep any food inside me after the high doses of Amisulpride, so weight was dropping off me without any effort on my part. It was not until T brought in some new clothes for me to wear that I realised. I had spoken to Annie about not having visitors and I knew my Mum and John wanted to visit. Annie said she would ring them to ask them to cancel but when the time came they visited anyway. The only reason why I didn't want visitors was because I always felt like I had to entertain and be OK for them and I couldn't do that in my current state which gave rise to more anxiety and worry. Ed rang me from the USA during the time when I couldn't really speak and when I came off the phone I just cried and cried as I felt I so much wanted to communicate with him as he means so much to me but couldn't get any words out. One of the first things I wanted to do when I could speak again was to give him a call. He has always been such a tower of strength for me in times of need along with his wife, B.

Three weeks into my stay I was becoming more stable but still felt physically under the weather and still struggling with Arthur but did not want my meds increased as I was scared of them after my bad experience of an increased dose. Dr R asked me if I would mind being a case study for a group of doctors and therapists at the hospital. I had been talking to a lady who worked in the therapy department who took me out for walks in Richmond Park on a daily basis where we would just walk and talk which became a great source of relief and pleasure for me. Other than this contact I hadn't engaged in any other group therapy as I still felt shaky both physically and mentally. Despite being fairly reclusive I agreed to talk to these doctors and agreed to meet Dr R at 10am outside the Blue Room – he said there would be about 20 people listening. He came out to get me at the allotted time and I entered the room. It was packed – I was petrified but I could see the therapist that I went walking with in the room so I focussed on her and sat it out. Dr R asked me questions as if I was in a consultation session with him and then opened the floor for questions. The first question came from another psychiatrist and was about my low weight, this was the first time that I considered my weight to have changed and never ever thought about it contributing to my condition. I was lost for words. The rest of the questions passed in a blur and I just remember leaving the room shaking and scuttled back to the sanctuary of my own cell.

Gloria was no longer with me full time after about 20 days and I felt safe shut away behind my door. I was by this time having visits from T or Mum or Dad most evenings and often went out with them for a change of scenery which I looked forward to each day. I needed to shave my legs so asked T if he could bring me a razor in as mine had been confiscated for my own safety. T did not know about my attempt at hanging myself but was aware I had used razor blades before to self harm. He said that he would bring one in if I promised not to do anything stupid. If I did he threatened to leave me. This put the fear of god into me and I made the promise. This however made it difficult for me as only a couple of weeks prior I had tried to kill myself and now I felt I couldn't tell him or he would leave me. I kept it all to myself. This was a turning point for me and I have never really self harmed since (bar the occasional scratch just to make myself feel better). I graduated to weekends out which I was petrified of as even after three weeks I had become quite institutionalised much to my horror. I was coping better though. I was taken to my room one day by Dr R and his colleague who sat me down to have the chat about how I would never be able to have children if I was taking the meds that I was currently using. At the time this did not bother me in the slightest as T already has children and did not want any more anyway and I had no inclination to change that. It did wake me up in a way though to realise that I had a problem which differentiated me from a lot of people – a choice had been taken away.

I re-engaged with my mobile phone and started to contact the outside world. I started to ring my mother on a daily basis and grew to look forward to our evening conversation, something that continues to this day. I was discharged at the end of November which is always a bad month for me (for some reason – dark, cold and short days?). I was on a high though and very restless – something that I enjoyed. I had got into a pattern of waking up at about 4am every morning and not being able to rest which left me quite tired and struggling to keep control but the euphoria of having boundless energy soon made up for this inconvenience.

Chapter 13

Ed was working on a magazine producing a monthly article of bizarre news called 'Needham's Believe it or Not'. Because it had my surname in the title I was able to show it to friends and show case my big brothers talents. I was so proud that Ed could be so visible even though this was early days in his magazine career. His career progressed from magazine contributor to Editor of FHM. He was very successful and was asked to become editor and launch FHM in the USA.

This would mean a move to New York which was exciting but also I had a tinge of disappointment as I felt I was just getting into his life albeit on the periphery. Ed's life in New York was successful and he went from being the editor of FHM to the editor of the institution of American magazines, Rolling Stone, and then finally the editor of Maxim, before returning to London to set up his own business.

It was whilst in New York however that I cemented my relationship with Ed and B. We spent long summer evenings (into the early morning) on the roof terrace of their apartment talking and building a close relationship. With a backdrop of the music of Nick Cave, 'Into my

Arms' has become an anthem associated with good times. This special time spent with Ed and B was a dream come true for me – being in the company of my big brother and feeling part of his life. This of course meant being part of B's life as well which was an added bonus as she has become someone who I can trust with everything and rely on an honest response. We had plenty of red wine flowing and managed to talk about the family and the relationships within the family and how we felt about the whole wife swap extravaganza. Also the environment was conducive to honesty and openness and for the first time with someone in my family had I spoken about my illness in detail and with respect in return. I felt safe so I could face the voices that were driving me to silence but the situation was too precious to let slip by – I may never have another chance. When I was speaking, with the help of the wine, I felt accepted and understood. There were many questions which in usual company I would have hedged and shut down but the time was right and the feeling was safe – I was winning – swimming with my head above water. In return both Ed and B were honest with me which made me feel a part of their lives, their busy lives which I felt I could only dream about becoming a part of. The short spell that I stayed in New York was so special; I had gained a brother and sister on a level that was far beyond any expectation or hope. When it came to my time to leave Ed hugged me which brought tears to my eyes. I have rarely experienced such warmth and especially not from a family member, this was the beginning. At the airport I was waiting for the plane which was delayed and more than once felt like turning and running back to Hudson Street and the roof terrace – it felt like

I belonged. On the plane home tears stained my face as I felt both happy at my experience and sad that I was leaving it behind (only in distance). It was a turning point in my life where I became able to identify and speak about emotions without feeling paralysed by fear by them.

The physical distance between Ed and I was made real to me when I was in the Priory at Roehampton, a hospital that I was to beginning to know well, as this was for a second inpatient spell. I had been over prescribed some new medication as a desperate attempt to change how I was feeling after an attempt at hanging myself in my hospital room. I was at an all time low and felt totally isolated and scared by the voices and hallucinations that I was experiencing. The new medication was strong and the dose increased daily until I was physically sick from it. My muscles seemed to seize up and I could not sit my self up in bed or move freely. Another side effect was that I lost the ability to speak freely as my mouth and muscles seemed to be unable to connect with the messages I was trying to send them from my brain. I received a treasured phone call from Ed in New York but was really unable to communicate with him as my speech just would not work. I just cried down the phone desperate to explain to him what the problem was. The call ended and I was devastated but also quite out of it with all the medication. As I came off some of the meds my speech and movements returned to normal but I had no outgoing phone at the hospital in my room. All I wanted to do was call Ed back and explain that I was OK but he seemed so far away. I had to attend therapy groups and was out of my room during the day when I was well enough to do so and missed a call from Ed during one of these times. I needed to speak to him. Eventually he managed to get hold of me and all was well. I could communicate again and felt safer with the knowledge that he was still there on my side. I was so sorry that I may have pushed him away by my lack of communication the first time he called – that would be too much to lose.

The next stage on building my family was when T came to New York with me to see Ed and B. T was nervous about meeting them but Ed and B were great and accepted him with their total hospitality and care that I had grown to know from them. This was such a change from the image that I had of Ed when I was a child of him shutting the world out. He was so engaging with sharp conversation the trip could not have gone better. I even got T to wear a pink shirt in the tradition of the family!!! We were all one.

Ed and B stayed in New York for many years, I lose count, and I made sure I visited them at least once every twelve months for my refill of summer nights on the roof terrace. These visits were made even more special however when their family was made complete with the adoption of Stella. Ed and B went through a rigorous and emotional journey in order to adopt Stella but looking at it from my viewpoint today, Stella was worth every minute of fretting and stress – it is easy for me to say!! Stella in my eyes brought yet another side of Ed into the daylight. His love and fun that he afforded Stella are second to none and this is yet another facet of his complex personality that attracts warmth from others. This warmth that was so well hidden in years gone by has risen to the surface and made him even more special in my heart. As I have said I would love to be like Ed and still harbour this wish as he continues to pull rabbits out of the hat. With Ed being much more expressive and open it has made it easier for others to see what I know – that he is such a wonderful, caring guy. The more people know this the better. Why would you want to hide such qualities? His loyalty to the family,and his honesty within it have been something that I have learnt from and continue to do so, and I thank Ed for that. He has made me realise that to get anywhere in life you have to be honest and prepared to take risks to say what I am really experiencing and thinking.

His wife B is another inspiration to me encouraging me to be true to myself and to set down in words the trials and excitements in my life so far and to leave no stone unturned. In their years in New York I can remember nights on the roof garden talking about my struggles and feeling completely accepted for who I am for what felt like the first time in my life. People had always been there for me but it was a realisation that I could be myself and was worth something dawned on me in those nights slurping the red wine and admiring the Manhattan skyline. Another addition to Ed and B's life is daughter little Stella Star who makes me smile just to think of her! As I am not going to have children of my own – as recommended by my psychiatrist when I was hospitalised and also because my husband T already has a grown up family and grandchildren who I love to bits as well – happy substitutes to make up with my lack of children of my own. Ed and B are the closest to a total package for me. I have told them everything about my experiences and feel that I can talk to them about all aspects of my illness with total acceptance and feeling. In fact it has become such a common topic of conversation – 'How are you?' they expect a proper response rather than just 'OK'. I know I can tell them exactly how I feel without feeling that I am over burdening them with details they are not interested in. To feel accepted and not judged is a gift that they have given me which has made it easier for me to open up to others as well.

Ed, B and Stella moved back to London recently which was fantastic as it means that they are closer to home and easier to communicate with and visit, although as usual when friends are on the doorstep you never see them as often as you could. Being twenty minutes away on the train however has set me the challenge of visiting and travelling on my own which has always been a challenge. I have yet to do it! I love the fact that they are there if I was to need them for any reason – it makes my world safer.

Chapter 14

This is what I wait for! The unannounced arrival of a good day is always something to look forward to. To wake up early with seemingly boundless energy starts the day as I hope it will go on. On such days the feelings of motivation and happiness return which makes me feel warm and human again. I want to go out all the time, restless when inactive. Easily bored in this state I tend to pace around the house unable to relax or sit down. Reading is out of the question as concentration spans five minutes if that. The television is usually ruled out as I get very scared if it starts to talk to me. Apart from these feelings I usually decide that I am 'better'. I resent taking medications when in this state as I do not want to change how I am today - I want to hold on to the good days.

There is always the concern that this 'fast forward' lifestyle will revert to a darker day tomorrow – just as unannounced as the good days. The 24 hour adrenaline rush that keeps me excited and happy all day, unable to slow down and unable to rest or sleep – like a child at Christmas I look forward to everything and feel totally revitalised and ready to take on any challenge. This carefree attitude helps to give me more confidence and a general boost in all areas of my life. That is what hurts more when the sunshine fades and I return to being haunted by voices and the lady that follows me around.

Endless cans of diet coke and cups of strong espresso are a way of trying to induce a 'high' but unfortunately I only get the restless and anxious kind of feelings that are fairly short lived and not as rewarding as a period of real happiness and excitement. Sometimes this fake 'high' is enough to remind me though that good times are just around the corner.

Things are never all that straight forward. When I walk down the street there is a presence. I cannot describe what that experience is like. I am still trying to understand this myself so that I can find out who I am.

I have never seen anyone follow me – it is a sensation that starts deep inside me, clamminess, a chill. A compulsion to spin my head around wildly to catch people out who are lingering in my shadow – I try to avoid too many sudden movements as I believe that that would alert others to my predicament – it is a matter just for him and me.

I can't hear him and I can't see him but I know the way he moves and his silent blanket which engulfs me – this is always worse in the evenings and at night – I do not think he is a morning person.

I need to divert, to change course, to shake off the enemy in my wake. If I am driving I can choose a different route and continue to do so until I feel all danger has been averted and I no longer feel that washing machine feeling – my stomach spinning like a tumbler. If I am walking I need to be ready to run at any given signal – it is tempting just to run any way, to escape, but I must stay anonymous to the world (that means that nobody knows me). A calm exterior but racing inside.

Some days the presence is no longer and although the memory remains the realism has faded into the unbelievable – can it really have been that scary? Of course there was no one there! I feel stupid explaining to people after the event how I had felt during a period under chase – how do you portray that intensity and fear without people thinking you are a crazy? I do not tell people any more – at first I wanted people to know as I thought this may stop the presence in his own tracks but this failed. It only received raised eyebrows or indulgent 'well never mind . . . lets brush it under the carpet' type remarks.

Every day he visits me. I believe that he is related to Arthur but is not Arthur. It is difficult to believe they are not connected as both seem to have the same aim of extinguishing me. If they are unconnected there must be something drastically wrong with me to have two men out to crumble me – why me? I hate people who say that – 'why me?' Self pity does no one any favours - just try a bit of denial for a change!!!

It helps to make a joke of it as people can laugh about a subject such as Arthur or the Presence without going out of their comfort zone. I find that when pushed into facing what I am saying about seeing and hearing people my audience becomes uneasy not knowing what to say – best keep it light hearted – brush it under the carpet again (I think I probably am guilty of this on far too many experiences in my time).

This is something that shapes my life as I have to spend my time managing myself to avoid situations of fear. People scare me, as does being alone. A no win situation may be seem but there are ways around it.

One way is if I can keep safe people around me like T, Mum, Ed, B – in fact all my family members (including especially Olive and Roxy, my two Bassett hounds, who always look after me). If there are too many people about I do not know who is really there and who is not and I can become quite intimidated by this. My reaction is either to stay silent and near a safe person, or to take a risk and totally bluff it by going out of my way being 'chatty'. I know this is what people expect of me (often people have said 'what's the matter with Lu? She is very quiet') and if I go along with this I can experience a nervous adrenaline rush which gets me through the evening or event.

Sometimes after a glass or two of wine this bravado can be quite fun but nearly always after the event, when I am in bed that night, I replay the evening to assess and check out the risks that I took and how dangerous the situation may have been. Also I can acknowledge having some fun interacting although I am usually suspicious of this.

Quite often if I know I have an event looming I will plan certain conversation pieces that I feel I can cope with,

with anyone in a one on one situation. This way I am in control. I believe my fear escalates if I do not feel in control of the situation.

In contrast being without people also scares me and fills me with a sense of fear. Close people such as T or family members I cannot imagine being without and often wonder what I would be like without them. I know this is the case for most people although if I am having a low spell in my mood these thoughts often come into my mind leaving me feeling very sad and emotional.

Despite these fears I know I can survive. I am aware that I can be resilient if I need to be as it is important always for me to 'hold it together'. If I show emotion too readily I perceive this to be a weakness (I know logically this is not the case but getting this from logic to feeling and believing seems to be difficult). I have a determination to do everything as well as I can and when I am sure of what I want I can usually focus quite well on getting there. I believe going through four back operations and suffering from mental illness problems this has strengthened my resolve to get through things no matter how scary they may be.

Fear can be used as a motivator as well as something that paralyses. In each extreme I have learnt that both can be used to my benefit. Manipulating, maybe, just to make myself comfortable which is what it is all about for me – finding a comfort zone to live within. I think my comfort zone is widening as I become more confident in a range of situations and I am not as paranoid. Five years ago it was almost impossible to feel comfortable in any situation, even in our home, without a nagging fear. Now, thanks to my close people, I have learnt to be OK with some situations, which is a huge relief for me (and, I believe, for those who have stuck by me to pick up the pieces). More recently I heard a description of threat and fear. Fear was described to me as being a healthy warning system that everyone experiences at times. This fear only becomes a problem if you have to act on it – that is when it becomes a threat. For example, if I was in the house alone and heard a noise downstairs the initial fear or warning would be aroused. This only becomes an active threat if I get up and see a stranger in the house having broken in – I have to respond to the fear in the form of a threat. The message to me was that fear is normal, threat is the problem but this only materialises in a minimum number of actual circumstances. In theory I can follow this suggestion. In practice – well that is something different!!!

I sometimes see a lady with an axe and to my knowledge, from feedback of others, they do not see her. She used to frighten me rigid as I believed she was going to use the axe to kill me. (That is what Arthur said). However she has never attacked me and is still around me a lot of the time. With persuasion from people with whom I shared my experience, I have come to believe that the lady is on my side. I treat her as my guardian angel and feel reassured when she is about in times of paranoia and confusion. This seems a simple change from negative to positive but it takes me a long time to trust but she has earned it. I am happy to have her about. She has not got a name as I believe she is part of me that is a protective part unlike Arthur who is external and intrusive when not welcome.

This is what I believe and that is important for me to have strong beliefs to hold on to. Fear is a big part of my life but as I said earlier it has strengthened me with more resolve to get through it and in time I know fear will have no negative effects but just a strong motivation to go straight through it. What a relief that would be!

Chapter 15

2003 to 2005 was filled with fantastic trips, spells of fainting, being a guinea pig in trials of a new drug and having batteries fitted into my body.

In 2003, T landed a voluntary position in the Lawn Tennis Association as Chairman of International and Professional Tennis. This role was highly prized as it meant that the holder of the position and his partner were invited to all the Davis Cup matches (GB men v other international teams) around the world as well as the female equivalent and other tennis events in far flung places. Much like my tennis days part of the excitement came from having to go where the teams were drawn to play – not always places you would choose to travel to so new experiences were almost guaranteed!

For my first foray into Davis Cup tennis (T had previously held the position 10 years earlier), the GB men drew to play Australia in Sydney. What a fantastic start! The tickets were booked for us business class (which T upgraded to First Class as he thought he would never have such an opportunity again). This added to the excitement for me. The fixture also coincided with my birthday at the beginning of February. We were all set.

I went to Cambridge to see some friends the day before our flight and was due to come back after having dinner with my Mum. In the afternoon however it started to snow quite heavily so I decided to set out back home at 3pm to ensure I was back alright. I got 5 miles down the road and was stuck in traffic and snow was falling heavily. I was not too worried as I thought it would just be until I got on to the main dual carriageway that would be for the bulk of my journey. I phoned T from the car to say where I was and that I May be delayed, but that was it as my mobile phone was running low on battery charge. 4 o'clock passed, then 5 o'clock, then 6 and I called T again to say that I would be very late but was sure I would make it through. I was starting to worry though. I was sitting in a queue and the snow was covering all my windows so I couldn't see anywhere. The traffic moved slowly and even when I reached the motorway the whole road was jammed. I took a back road and I crawled to the next town and came off to try to go the back way home. Many people had the same idea and more people seemed to be joining the throng. I got to a slope that I needed to climb but cars were not able to get up so we were jammed in a fix where it was difficult to get out. I was getting stressed but decided to try a u-turn which worked but to where next? I decided to try to go to a 24 hour food store but they were shutting at 10pm so the best I could do was to use their phone to call T and tell him I was still on my way but was heading back to the motorway. Got back to the motorway, it was still jammed solid. Across the road from the entrance to the motorway was a hotel. I decided to go there and thought I could set out later when things had cleared. I used the hotel phone to call T and he was unsure what to do as we had to be at the airport early the next morning for our flight to Oz. I spent a few hours in the hotel and then at 4am decided to try again. I rang T and said I would try again and as I was leaving the hotel a man came up to me to ask if he could get a lift as his heavily pregnant wife was stuck in traffic further down the road. The motorway was now moving. It was a strange night and for some reason I gave the guy a lift. So here I was crawling down the icy but now empty motorway at 4am with a strange man sitting next to me! I eventually got to my exit and the man got out determined to walk the rest of the way. It was still freezing cold but had stopped snowing so off he went! I still had a tricky journey ahead. It was only a few miles but on smaller roads that were badly affected by the snow. I chose a route that was slightly longer but avoided steep slopes and after a hairy hour or so I arrived home at 6am. I got through the door and shouted for T but no reply. Upstairs fast asleep!!! So much for an anxious partner!!

I woke him up and we left straight away for the airport still hopeful that we could make it. The taxi company taking us to the airport said they couldn't because of the weather. We took our car. Locally the roads were snow laden and difficult, however as we got to the M25 the road was clear and no traffic so we made good time. It seemed crazy after the night I had had that the roads were now clearer. It was a triumph for me as I had been all night travelling with my doubts but made it through when I had to, which showed I could do things alone if I really was pushed to it. I did not want to go through anything like that again though!

This meant that we arrived in the First Class lounge at Heathrow Terminal 4 in time for a few hours wait for a delayed flight.

I soon became quite at home with the idea of ordering food and drink at no charge and made up for Thursdays diet of carrot cake and kettle chips by munching my way through soup and salad. Things were looking up. Patience was thinning when the flight boarded 4 hours later than advertised, but the novelty of first class and fully reclining seats and a glass of champagne soon assuaged any feelings of stress. Ready now for lunch again (the third one today!) and a long sleep through to Singapore – the next stage of my journey.

Arrived in Sydney 3 hours late and caught a cab to the Four Seasons hotel. Very chatty cabby – typical Ozzy rambling about how good everything Australian is compared to England's crap cricketers and lacking tennis stars. The hotel is very nice in a very busy area on the waterfront in Sydney. It is Saturday night. No room was booked for us - they seemed to think we were arriving tomorrow so we will have to change rooms after one night. From tomorrow we are in a 'junior suite'. Went out for a cigarette but everywhere was heaving with people so we trudged back to floor 17 for a room service pizza at midnight. Exploration begins tomorrow.

Sunday 1st February, 2003

Woke up at 5am and read etc until 8.30am. Columbia space shuttle blew up – bad luck! Opened the day with a stroll to the harbour to see Sydney Harbour Bridge and the Opera House which was smaller than I had imagined and not silver. Even so I took lots of pictures. The market stalls along the front were first class so I promised to buy myself a hat on the way back.

We strolled into the Botanic Gardens to see the bat trees. Beautiful open spaces surrounded us full of emptiness among the trees. Found the bat trees and took more pictures. Nice day beginning to get hot. We decided to go on the ferry to Manly. Got the ferry and spent 30 minutes crossing the water in a large boat with about 1100 passengers – some of whom were very fat but still persisted on eating for Australia. Manly was busy, with a nice surfing beach, although the whole area was a bit Southendesque. We had lunch sitting near the beach talking to two Lakeland terriers who were sitting at the next table. The meal portions were humongous – I thought I would be travelling back on the ferry looking like the fat family who we saw on the way out!

Back to the hotel for a move to a new room. Much nicer a suite – aren't we important!? After a cigarette and a coke we set off again into the Rocks area – a great place with lively markets and music everywhere. Managed to buy everything I needed on the way along the market including a present for Janet and a lorry for James and Nicholas. Began to get hungry and tired so stopped off for a Starbucks for a coffee and brownie – diet out of the window again today. Time for a kip before dinner – dead tired!! Jet lag strikes.

We went out in the evening towards the Rocks for an Italian dinner very nice. Rain came down whilst eating but cleared up later. Why are there no illuminations lighting up the Sydney Opera House at night? We are going to visit the Blue Mountains tomorrow.

Monday

We went to breakfast to meet Charles (LTA President), Stuart (Deputy President) and Marilyn his wife. A little bit nervous as have never really met them before and I am not quite sure what to expect. No problem though as they were not there!!!

Gathered stuff together and T organised a hire car (Mitsubishi not Mazda) and drove to Katoomba in the Blue Mountains which was about a 2 hour drive. Quite OK though as no steep drops at the edge of the road that I had been worried about. Arrived in Katoomba and went for coffee in a drag bar – no one on show at 11.30am though!!

Decided to head for Echo Point. Very grey and drizzly in Katoomba especially as I was only wearing shorts and a sun top – absolutely freezing. It was so cold I hit the gift shop immediately to buy a sweat shirt to keep warm. With Australia emblazoned across my chest I was now the true tourist! We took the customary pictures and stood well back from the edge to view the Three Sisters rock formation. Spectacular but a long way down!! We decided to head for lunch at Wentworth Falls which turned out to be another quiet cowboy type town just on the way back towards Sydney. Like tourists we headed for the viewpoint of the falls. Again very spectacular but not much water in the falls – there was more falling out of the sky!

We headed back for Sydney via McDonalds and Homebush tennis stadium where the match would be played at the end of the week. As we had the car we decided that we would drive across Sydney towards Watsons Bay. Very nice area of town with spectacular views (seem to have seen a lot of them today!) back across Sydney Harbour. Drove on to Bondi which had big waves but was Bondi beach was a relatively small beach which surprised me – I expected a large expanse of golden sand and not an elongated cove!! Very nice sand though and glad to see it. Drove back to George Street via Oxford Street – a shopping street in Sydney that was on my itinerary for later in the week but has since been crossed off as it is a very seedy and tacky area – wouldn't see that in Manhattan!

We strolled around the harbour again looking for Diet Coke and a cowboy hat for T. Found one and he looks great! Also located Doyles on the Quay that was to be our eating establishment later on that evening. Were accompanied to dinner by Charles, Gavin, Marilyn and Stuart for an enjoyable evening of gossip, and more importantly a big plateful of John Dory – very nice too! Back to the hotel to get some rest for tomorrow. Taronga Zoo on the cards along with an art gallery with Marilyn and a beer with Tree (A friend of Ed and B who is working in Australia). (Also my birthday – Don't forget!!).

Tuesday
Happy Birthday to me.

The day opened with a boat trip to Taronga – Fantastic zoo. Lovely sunny day and really warm. Plenty of animals on view. Best animals were giraffes and koalas. All animals had spacious enclosures and seemed to be quite relaxed. Taronga is one of the better zoos that we have seen on our travels. We do tend to check them out wherever we are on our trips. The sky train helped us down to the ferry again with the customary spectacular views across the harbour (The bridge and Opera House were on view – better than room 7015!)

Lunch on Circular Quay was great and very relaxing with a good atmosphere. Got worried about the afternoon ahead with Marilyn but it turned out that there was no need. We walked through the Botanic Gardens to the Art Gallery of NSW to see the Picasso exhibition. The guide was fantastic filling on stories around the paintings. Very informative and brought the afternoon to life. We walked back to the hotel to meet the men who had been to watch the practice at the tennis. Marilyn described me as being strange and that she had never met anyone like me before!!!!

Met Tree for a V & T in the hotel bar – very nice person, full of life and definitely an individual! Really pleased to meet her. Dinner was at Aria – a very posh restaurant overlooking the harbour (it seems that there are very few places that we have been in Sydney that do not overlook the harbour!). Great fish dinner to round off the day. Sat next to John Crowther (C.E at LTA) and had a good chat – burnt lots of calories via nervous tension!

Tomorrow is Darling Harbour and a didgeridoo shop for Martin Corries Birthday.

What a great day!!

Wednesday

Woke up very early again but after a much better night's sleep – breakfast in the room today which was much better as well.

Walked to Darling Harbour – much hotter today. Went to the aquarium and watched the seals being fed and had a chat with two seals that were sunbathing. Another lovely seal was wriggling on his back in the sun. Very loveable. Also loveable were the tiny penguins, but not so loveable were the many varieties of shark floating about.

After the aquarium the shops were our next target. Across the bridge, that came apart whilst we were crossing, the shops were a little bit disappointing. Lunch was lovely back at the hotel and then a quick stroll into The Rocks to a couple of art galleries. The artist Ken Dome provided me with a fantastic t-shirt about butterflies with no voice, and tomorrow I will go back to buy a print for Mum. Next door the Egan Gallery had 10 cards for $10 so that couldn't be missed – another bargain!! Also on our shopping list in The Rocks was a didgeridoo for Martin. They were everywhere so that was no problem.

Back to the hotel for a sleep – very nice, and then a pre-afternoon coffee swim. Jacuzzi lovely – swimming pool was unheated and very cold. During the morning the wind had picked up and was blowing a gale.

Off for a coffee which was great watching the world go by on George Street. Then back up the street to buy a skirt which I saw earlier. Such a greedy shopper never missing a bargain of course!

Dinner tonight is at Watsons Bay – Doyle's on the Beach. T has organised a water taxi not knowing that Stuart hates being on water. I think it is quite exciting, and I hope everyone enjoys it. Sometimes I feel responsible for everyone else having a good time – just something else to worry about. Will report back tomorrow how the evening went.

"If you see a turtle sitting on top of a fence post, it didn't get there by accident" Bill Clinton, 1998.

Not sure the significance of this quote but it seemed good at the time.

Thursday

Last night at Doyle's was fantastic. We got the water taxi and left behind views of the harbour, with the sun going down, whilst speeding out to Watsons Bay. The fish was fantastic too and the place appeared to be a British enclave with Cliff Richard, Sue Barker and Parkinson sitting close by. A quick trip back on the water taxi rounded the evening off especially for Stuart who appeared to be petrified! You have to face your fears sometime!

This morning began with a trip to the Museum of Contemporary Art on the quay. Great exhibition but very strange that left me feeling a bit freaked out (especially the half head and the giant naked pregnant woman!).

Lunch was with Tree and Leyla (a tennis friend on holiday in Australia) at Sailors Thai in The Rocks. One long table down the centre of the room but the food was marvellous. Post prandial Tree went back to work (maybe I won't see her again?) and we went to Darling Harbour for a trip on the monorail around the area. The monorail was great but obviously too good as it was packed with people 'doing the loop' so it was difficult to see out of the windows. Coffee and coke at the aquarium followed, and then a boat trip (The Rocket) back to Circular Quay. Another V&T later in the bar did me for the day so time to prepare for the evening. A night out of low key early eating with the LTA gang who were good fun if you wanted to talk about tennis!

Tomorrow the tennis starts which is a relief as the build up has seemed to be interminable – the players must be going barmy. Can't wait. Bus leaves at 8.30am.

Friday

Got up early to catch the bus to the tennis at 8.30am. It didn't come! Got a car at 9am to the tennis at Homebush and arrived shortly before the opening ceremony at 9.45am. The court looked fantastic, very red and soft looking. Sadly we do not have best players Tim and Greg, they are both injured.

Play started and Alan Mackin put up a good fight against Phillipoussis but could not match the Aussies power or standards. After a brief lunch we went for more toasting by the court. Thank god for Diet Coke and also thank god I am not a man having to wear a jacket and tie. The Barmy Army were out in full force (they go everywhere) dressed in red t-shirts and Union Jack baseball caps and made a good bit of noise but nothing to match the yellow Australian Fanatics complete with drums, trumpets, bagpipes and very loud voices. Alex Bogdanovic lost to Hewitt.

The funniest incident was when one of the Australian supporters came into the stand wearing a dress and a mask of the Queen. The crown all stood and bowed it was really hilarious.

We had a cup of tea with Stuart and Marilyn when back at the hotel chewing over the day's goings on – tennis in general. I think that they thought I was odd as I kept finishing T's sentences filling in missing names! I also think that Marilyn was very bored discussing tennis yet again!

Off to The Rockpool restaurant tonight for dinner. I hope Gwen and Mike (LTA Sponsors) are coming as they are really interesting people to talk to and they have a puppy always a good topic for dog owners.

Just doubles tomorrow starting at 10am, so I guess another early bus ride which is beginning to seem earlier every day as I begin to acclimatise to the Aussie time. I am sure I will survive. I must also try not to get too burnt tomorrow which is very easy sitting in a sunny stand all day. Also seem to have been eating all day. Porker!

Went to Rockpool for dinner with the LTA group and the British Consol. Great restaurant – more tasty fish. Decided not to drink tonight with the exceptance on one

V.A.T. but it didn't work too well as I followed up my relatively alcohol free evening with the worst nights sleep that I have had so far. Better luck tomorrow.

Saturday

Doubles only today at the tennis and then tonight the Official Dinner.

Phillipoussis did not play the doubles but Woodbridge and Hewitt just held it together after an appalling start by our boys Maclagan and Parmar in the first two sets.

After the tennis yesterday we strolled as usual looking for the markets but they only appear on Sunday so to no avail. Then a sleep before the Official Dinner. More luck with the markets tomorrow lets hope the tennis is not too extended.

Sunday

I got a bit worried about the Manly ferry last night. I had an inkling that it would get to just outside Circular Quay and then sink. So I was quite worried all last night and had to get up to see if I could see any trace of it in the harbour. I believe my worries were eventually unfounded which was a huge relief.

Off to the tennis again today after last night's dinner in the Ballroom at the hotel. I sat next to a very rough and self centred ex player called Mark Edmonson who seemed quite disappointed that I didn't know of him! I don't think he has ever been popular. The rest of the table were all made up of ex-Davis Cup players for

Australia, all of whom seemed really nice. Thank god it is over though!

Tennis today will be OK with two short dead rubbers. I hope Phillipoussis plays as I was quite in awe of his power and would like to watch it again.

I am sitting in the window of our 7th floor room at 6.30am writing this and watching people swim in the pool below, with a view over the Harbour and Opera House. I think I will miss it as it has been a fantastic trip that I will never forget. One day to go!

Monday

Yesterday the tennis was entertaining and reasonably successful. Miles played Wayne Arthurs to begin with and lost in three sets putting up a good show, followed by Bogo playing Todd Woodbridge (that well known singles player) as no other Australian wanted to play. Bogo went on to win which was fantastic and deserved.

After the tennis, a trip around The Rocks market was in order, although for some reason we were both ready to go to sleep!! Back to the hotel, where we met Roger Taylor (GB Davis Cup Captain) in the bar. It was something that seemed to be becoming a daily ritual. He was pleased with his team and rightly so. After putting British tennis to rights for the eighth day in succession it was time to crash out in the room for a while.

Dinner yesterday was at an Italian in The Rocks which was good fun. T seemed to have the spotlight placed on him for some reason as I was asked to highlight his good points which are numerous. He was then quizzed on his lifestyle which I believe everyone else around the table was quietly impressed by, wishing they had had the ability and foresight to have led such a life. I love him!!

Today, Monday, is our last day which I am quite sad about although I think we have exhausted Sydney for this trip anyway. Going back to the cold and wet of England doesn't fill me with joy although I guess some things will be good but I can't quite put my finger on them yet! I am looking forwards to going back to my counselling class as it seems an age since I was there, and I am also looking forward to seeing Caroline, Janet and Jane who are all good friends.

The car comes at 2.30pm to take us to the airport so the morning will be spent drinking coffee and preparing to go home!!

We wandered around the shops lethargically – neither of us seemed to have too much energy so we stopped for the usual coffee and decided to go back to the hotel. I slept for an hour or so before being rudely awakened by the telephone asking us to vacate our room! The car to the airport was on time and check in was early with us being escorted to the lounge by a thin girl with a pointed nose and strange make-up. Looking forward to sleeping on the plane!

The trip from Sydney to Bangkok was uneventful. I slept a lot, the food was poor and T broke his chair and got grumpy!! It was marginally more exciting from Bangkok to Heathrow as Brian May and Anita Dobson made their way into the first class cabin. Brian was quite eye catching dressed in a long black jacket with his long black curly hair and very tall presence. So tall that he hit his head on an aptly named overhead locker!! Like the other passengers they slept all the way to London – or at least I did so I like to assume that everyone else did too!

I have thoroughly enjoyed this trip and meeting different people – which is strange as usually I can't think of anything that I would rather do less! I enjoyed meeting Tree and feeling like a friend, and also feel I was accepted by the other Brits abroad (despite Marilyn suggesting that '*I have never met anyone like you, you are rather strange aren't you?*'). There were daily discussions about tennis which were quite interesting although I don't know where they lead to – maybe just a means to an end? I even managed an afternoon alone with Marilyn which was what I was dreading before the trip. I didn't want to be a 'Davis Cup wife' . I have learnt a lot about others and myself, and feel that I would be able to do it again without quite so much dread!

Morocco will be our next Davis Cup venue.

We left Olive our dog – very sad but she seemed happy, and made our way to Heathrow. We arrived very early as I had spent all morning pacing around the house in my restless fashion. Hit the shops and nearly managed to pass the bookshops but was ultimately sucked in to buy a book about an alcoholic – something I want to know more about. This was only the beginning though and 400 Marlboros and two pairs of shoes later we boarded the flight with Charles. Uneventful flight with inedible food, which was to be a precursor for the week, so nearly managed to finish my Teddy Tinling book – great man very inspirational.

Arrived in Casablanca to be met by Gavin and some Moroccan guys who ushered us into a private lounge and plied us with sweet green mint tea – revolting! Bags were collected for us and passports checked whilst we were ensconced in the VIP lounge. Our driver negotiated the streets of Casa which were total chaos likened by T to the streets of Moscow – something that fortunately I have been unfortunate enough never to have experienced.

This week in Casablanca is the trial of a dual nationality Moroccan / British bomber and so there is a risk of attacks against British subjects.

The hotel is an oasis in the chaos of Casablanca and the rooms spacious. But before we were allowed to relax we were whisked away to a VIP lounge (which was to become a free bar during the week) for an orange juice with Dennis Healy from the Consulate. Formalities over, it was into the bar for a beer with dinner to follow avoiding the Moroccan restaurant on this occasion. It was a lively bunch of people for dinner with Charles, Stuart, Derek, John C, Gavin, T, Don (Security) and John Parsons. Interesting stories regaled by JP of his introduction to journalism at the age of 14 – very able man with great determination to succeed. I had underestimated him which steels me to be less judgemental in future – bad trait!

The first day over – time to sleep in our enormous bed. Feel quite safe as Don the security man for the GB Team assured us that the hotel is crawling with plain clothes policemen. I ask myself why? But instead of panicking at this early stage I am going to try to leave my wellbeing to those around me – I guess they know best. Always a dodgy assumption.

Wednesday 16-09-03

Breakfast in room on eighth floor – very nice + chat to Roger, I think his chest gets bigger every time we meet! Out to the tennis to see the place and the team practice – pretty hot but at least the transport had brakes this time unlike the ride from the airport where it was definitely metal on metal! We sat through a press conference with the Brits and two men and a dog. Watched practice for a while - men with no shirts! Arazi wins the vote for best body but is very arrogant–The one I have my eye on is El Aynoui!!

Sat by the pool all afternoon and had a swim and a sleep.

Dinner was an occasion tonight as it was the official dinner. Had a chat to a Swiss lady who lives in Casablanca as we were the only two European women there. Dinner was horrific lumps of animals and unrecognisable accompaniments that Dennis Nilssen would have been proud of. The entertainment was a Moroccan lady singer in karaoke style who was somewhat unattractive. Towards the end of the evening the Moroccan players dressed in traditional white pyjamas started dancing and dragged up the Brits who in true British fashion looked as wooden as ever – the Africans won my vote for spontaneity – something I like and wish I had. Tomorrow is another day.

Thursday 17-09-2003

Morning tour around the mosque – 2nd largest in the world after Mecca in Saudi Arabia. Fantastic building from the outside, took loads of pictures. Will go back on Saturday for a tour inside. Then on to Habbous a new market area like the more modern medina. Lots of traders dealing in beautiful silver and ceramics with Moroccan dress also for sale. Saw a great child's dress for Gwen but did not buy it – only purchased one ceramic plate for Mum. Bartered Mr Morocco down to half his original asking price, very pleased with myself today!

Back to the oasis of the Hyatt for the draw. Lots of press there followed by a press conference with the British team – very noisy and boring! Spent the afternoon asleep by the pool which was very relaxing. Woke up to find all the sun beds had been removed to prepare for a party. T and I were stuck alone in the middle! From 5-8pm there was a meeting with the supporters of the GB team. Free t-shirts to be snapped up like hot cakes by some very strange gannets! Spoke to a few of the aptly named BATS (British Association of Tennis Supporters) who were just that! Dedicated to tennis in a commendable but mind boggling way

Dinner tonight was with the French speaking President of the Moroccan Tennis Federation – Mr Mjid. Pre dinner drinks lasted for 2 hours with glasses of practically straight gin! Got talking to Neil Harman from the press and had quite a good evening. Dinner was foul!

Friday 18-09-2003

Tennis started today with Tim playing the arrogant Arazi. Terrible tennis from GB shown up by touches of brilliance at times from Morocco. The stadium was half empty due to a complete lack of advertising due to security threats against British citizens as the Casablanca bomber was on trial this week and he held Moroccan – British dual citizenship. To avert possible friction the tie was not advertised. Lunch was supposed to be in the restaurant at the club, but as we only had 20 minutes between matches then it was difficult to fit in three courses!! We ordered a main course only and still left before it arrived!

Greg started well against El Aynaoui to raise the spirits a little but by the 5th set gamesmanship by Younes disturbed Greg from his 4th set roll and he never got back on equal terms. End of Friday 0-2 very disappointing.

BBQ by the pool to entertain the press was good. Managed to give John Lloyd a grilling which he took quite well in good spirits and we had a good evening accompanied by some raw chicken and the ever present hideous Moroccan music at a very loud volume.

Saturday 19-09-2003

Another hot day. Woke up late feeling rough with a sore throat so missed the early morning trip to the Mosque. Slept until the bus left at 11.30am to sit in the sun watching tennis – tough life! Lunch is in the restaurant again which was nearly edible when half a chicken was plonked down with potatoes and rice – no Atkins diet here!

Tennis started after the official presentation ceremony with Tim and Greg playing Arazi and A.N.Other from Morocco. The first set was decidedly twitchy but then we settled down to a comfortable 3-0 win. Tim still looked dodgy but Greg was OK.

A trip to the BBC offices at the top of the stadium was hotter than ever with everyone housed like battery hens in little glass boxes. Glad to be back out in the sun after that. Purchased a sweat shirt for US$10 to help the Moroccan community and returned to the hotel to sleep – no energy for swimming today. Dinner at 8.15pm in the hotels café M – very nice fish although nouveau cuisine so need biscuits to follow!!

Sunday 20-09-03

1-2 and all to play for. Arrived early at the tennis again – this time found an espresso stand so could at least have a strong coffee. Woke up with a very sore throat and feeling like really bad again but who cares? Tim started at 11am against El Aynaoui – played excellent tennis in a very long 4 set duel which he won. Bigger crowds today getting more vocal as the match got closer – very hot in the stadium today.

Lunch in 20mins is getting better! Failed in stealing the tablecloth but did swipe two more napkins to complete a set of four!! 3 mouthfuls of chicken and back to support Greg against Arazi. Brilliant start to take the first set 7-5 but looked absolutely knackered. Struggled through the second set to lose it 5-7 then lost a close third set finished under floodlights 6-7 after having 2 set points. Play was suspended until tomorrow. The highlight of the match was Arazi telling T to f... off for cheering Greg!! Got a lift back to the hotel with Dennis Healy and his driver Ahmed. Traffic unbelievable as Ahmed took the central position across the lanes and continued onwards oblivious.

No gin on floor 8 so had to make do with vodka – hardship! All drinks and snacks are free on this floor so no need to complain. Final dinner in the bar tonight – more strange food but at least we got chips.

Ordered an early morning call for 7.45am as we have to leave for the airport. Quite ready to go home. I don't like Morocco at all. It kind of gets to me that we always have security with us at all times. It makes me nervous that they may be expecting something to happen.

Monday 21-09-03
No early morning call materialised so got up late. Quick breakfast then off to the airport. Quick check in which was very nice then off to the duty free where I found the most marvellous shoes – very Moroccan with sequins and pointed – bargain of the week. The plane left on time and the captain promised to give us news of the Greg match as soon as he got it.

The week in review – I had high expectations coming to Morocco – a restful change and a new unstressed outlook ready to start again when I came home. In fact I felt quite nervy and unsafe due to all the hype and security around British tourists in Casablanca. Felt worried as to why we needed the extent of the security - what is going on? Being kept in the dark with my mind running riot as usual – not a recipe for relaxation. Enjoyed the sun and the company but doubt whether I will ever return to Casablanca.

We were dropping down the league tables and our next match was against Luxembourg. We have still not had a match at home.

Luxembourg was a match we were down to win easily. We had a good team and the opposition was more lowly ranked. I was having a few hang ups around the Davis Cup as I was worried about people in the stadium sitting behind me were a danger to me. I became preoccupied with the feeing that someone in the building would kill me today. I found this harder in Luxembourg as the stadium was indoors and closed in where at least in Casablanca and Sydney the matches were outdoors which did not seem quite so intimidating to me.

I went to Luxembourg ready to try to enjoy the break.
    On the first match day we watched the tennis for the day and I survived the arena. Uncomfortable with my back pain – still ongoing at this stage whilst being cared for by a pain management specialist in London and his like of pain killing injections; and uncomfortable due to my fear of the audience, I was glad for the end of the day.

At this time I was struggling a lot with my schizophrenia and had been put forward by Dr R for a trial of a new drug coming out called Aripiprazole. This study was being conducted by a group of psychiatrists at the Maudsley Hospital in London and not by my usual doctor. This transition of doctors at a time when I did not feel particularly stable was hard enough. Then to go through a plethora of questions, blood tests etc and also to be weaned off all the meds I had previously been on, with the exception of the anti depressants, made my life (that I hated anyway) even harder to live with.

The first evening in Luxembourg after play had finished we were standing talking to a member of the press who had travelled out with the team when suddenly I collapsed on the floor in a heap. The team doctors came to help and we put the short episode down to heat in the arena and my pain levels in my back. The team doctor did ask about medications but he did not know about the Aripiprazole as it was still in its trial stages. I travelled back to the hotel and felt a bit washed out but basically OK. After all this was not my first experience of collapsing. Ready for another day at the tennis tomorrow.

The second day at the tennis was doubles day and a lot shorter as it was just one match. I sat through it with all my usual anxieties of the arena and my pain levels and survived. We went back to the hotel for a quick sleep before the official dinner that evening. I got all glammed up for the event and went off to the venue. I never really relished these events where you have to be on your best behaviour but it was fun to be there in some ways as both teams and the players attended to make it more interesting. I collected a glass of champagne and promptly passed out in a heap on the floor again! What an entrance!! The doctor was there again and I was carried off to the changing rooms where the teams spend their days. I felt awful and we chatted about my back and pain levels and briefly about the drug trial but really were none the clearer. I was due to see both the pain specialist and the psychiatrist in charge of the drug trial on my return to London. I made it back via a wheelchair at the airports and a lot of support. The only good thing was that GB won 4-1 and got out of the Euro Africa Group again.

I visited the psychiatrist on my return and had more blood tests. I was walking back to his office when I fainted again. The consultant came but said it could not possibly be the drugs that were on trial as they do not have that side effect! I felt this was a fairly brave statement seeing as the drugs were on trial to establish any side effects or effects of any sort on the condition. T and I made a decision to stop the new trial drug. The fainting stopped. I returned to seeing Dr R who came up with a cocktail of anti depressants, anti psychotics and mood stabilisers. This eventually helped me back to a more stable state – more importantly where I could walk around without ending up as a heap on the floor!

I was still attending the pain specialist for my back pain which had not eased so I was in line for another scan and Epiduroscopy under anaesthetic to try for another few months grace. It did used to work temporarily – very temporarily (one or two months) but anything seemed positive at the time.

We moved onto Austria for the next match.

Fantastic place – Portschach in southern Austria on a beautiful lake in September. Mum and John came as well which was great and they had a fabulous time in between rain showers watching the tennis, boating on the lake and getting the train to nearby Klagenfurt for a bit of a change. We stayed in a lovely hotel a short walk away fron the tennis.

Tennis on wet red clay not ideal – we lost 2-3 in a match which transpired to be Henman's last Davis Cup appearance for his country.

We were now relegated to the Euro Africa zone again, this time against Israel in Tel Aviv. The people are all so kind and loving to each other and warmth was offered to us as guests. Security was tight as bombs were expected and a curfew was put onto the delegation not to leave the hotel in the evenings without security for 'our own safety'. One evening we were invited to the British Ambassadors house for dinner.

The wine flowed and my darling husband, sitting next to the young lady who was the Ambassadors assistant, brought up the subject of religion and 'what is all this kosher nonsense about?' They spent most of dinner discussing these things and T really enjoyed finding out about religion and Jewish food.. A good time was had by all.

Another evening we were entertained in a typically Israeli restaurant where courses of food kept coming all evening specially prepared for our party – again top class company and more wine flowed!! The tennis had highs and lows. Bogdanovic chosen in Henman's retirement as the number two singles player opened the show with a dismal performance lacking in application in an important rubber. Greg relished his role as senior team member and put in a professional performance to get us to 1-1. The decider was, without doubt, Saturdays doubles with Andy Murray (playing his first Davis Cup match) and David Sherwood thrown in a do or die effort to escape further relegation. Against a quality Israeli doubles pairing the adrenaline flowed and a momentous coming of age took place with the Brits coming through to win that match. Following that match we were going up in the lift at the hotel with Greg and talking about the next day's tennis. He said 'I should win my match in about 2 hours.' True to his word after 1 hour 45 mins, at the change of ends, preparing to serve for the match, he just looked across and smiled as if to say I told you so. It is not arrogance it is self belief which he had in abundance. Final result 3-2 GB.

We now go back to the World Group Play Offs – Roger Federer's Switzerland in Geneva. Again on Clay but this time indoors Murray was put to the test but was beaten by a higher ranked opponent who was the Swiss number 2. Federer was a joy to watch in his demolition job over Mackin and also in the doubles. It was a shame for the supporters that the Murray against Federer match never got played but who would guess that the following week they would meet each other in the ATP Bangkok final! We were well beaten 5-0.

I could not write about my Davis Cup experience without mentioning the B.A.T.S. – British Association of Tennis Supporters. At all the Davis Cup matches there has been a strong travelling posse of supporters with Union Jacks and hooters etc to urge their favourites on. A welcome party is arranged for them on the Thursday

before the match starts where there are drinks and
nibbles and free T-shirts (the real reason for travelling!)
As T's and my job was to distribute the freebies we have
become very popular in the BATS circles and have got
to know many of them. They are all mad and help
to make the Davis Cup special – they have been one
of the consistent highlights across all ties that I have
experienced.

The three years in office are over but I am pleased to say
my Davis Cup bug has not expired. The next tie is in
Glasgow against either Serbia Montenegro or Israel
again. Soon I will be an honorary BAT (I think T is their
elected LTA information supplier and LTA idol). What a
reputation to live up to.

Chapter 16

During these years of travel and trauma between 1999 and 2004 I embarked on a few mad cap ideas in a bid to make myself worthwhile and valid to others that knew me, but mostly to satisfy that ever present drive that leads me from challenge to challenge.

I was working at Marylebone Cricket Club (MCC) at Lord's Cricket Ground in London, in an office where women were considered second class citizens and are even barred from going in certain rooms in the building such as the precious 'Long Room'. The first week of work at the MCC I wore trousers and was quickly admonished that 'Ladies attend work in skirts'.

Life at the MCC was not challenging so I decided to enrol at Leicester University to do an MSc Masters degree in Forensic and Legal Psychology. This subject was chosen on the basis that my long term obsession with serial killers and their methods and psychology. The course was for two years and was entirely distance learning so I did not have to attend University on a daily basis.

The course was really interesting although time consuming, and I felt really out of my comfort zone having to write essays again. It was also difficult to concentrate and focus on all the reading even though I loved the subject. The stress continued and I had a down turn in health that made me take the decision to defer year 2 for twelve months.

The twelve months passed very quickly and when it came to my re-admission to the course I was full of self doubt. In year 2 I had the usual monthly essays and also a 10,000 word dissertation. I wrote the beginning of my dissertation on 'Violent behaviour as a result of closed head injuries'. I was in the Priory for my first stay at this time. It was a good way of distracting myself from the reality of being stuck in a mental hospital for a third year running.

I completed my dissertation with a sigh of relief and sent it off to my tutor. It came back with a few suggestions which I duly corrected. – job done.

It was a relief to complete the Masters but soon after I was itching for more. I was now doing a faceless job working in the Tennis Office in Hertfordshire. The people were great but I could not cope with a lot because of my mental condition so I only worked 3 days a week.

Soon I wanted another challenge! I enrolled on a Postgrad Counselling Diploma and attended the first week at night school in Cambridge. My health was not good though and I was admitted to the priory for a second time. I was away from the course until week 10, I turned up and they allowed me to continue. I then attended every Thursday evening and most weekends for 4 years.

I did a lot of talking, writing, video role play and assessments to get through the first three years of my diploma course. The time and commitment from me to do this was full on despite it only being a part time course. I found myself asking questions about myself and also Annie really helped me along the way as she was also keen for me to explore myself to find revelations (rather than answers).

I got to the stage where I needed to get a placement to practice and hone my skills in the real world. I was lucky and with the support of the course leaders managed to secure an interview and subsequently a placement working with drug and alcohol addictions on a one to one and on a group basis within a day centre for people with addictions, this was with Vale House Rehabilitation Centre. The team there were fantastic and I learned vast amounts which made the course more bearable as it rolled on towards the end. I found that having a placement and working with 'real' people made the whole counselling concept come alive for me. I worked as a volunteer for two days a week and made sure that I tallied up enough hours to qualify that summer. All my written and assessed exam work was completed and so I just needed to keep working at the placement. I had no intention of doing anything different. I loved working with the client group I was ensconced in with many high and low points. We had clients that we saw off to rehab for 6 months to return free of their vice. On the other hand some young people could not cope with their demons and lost the battle – this was the hardest part of the role.

I found, that having been through hardships and was still going through very real and emotional mental health issues of my own, it did help me to fit in with the client group I was working with. I never disclosed my personal position with the clients but hoped that they felt that I understood and could support them in a knowing way.

What I was doing cannot have been too bad as when I had received my counselling qualifications, the head of the unit offered me a paid job in the North Hertfordshire Probation Area, which was an area they also controlled.

My paid job would be to work with offenders who had drug and alcohol problems linked to their offending behaviour. I snapped the job out of her hand as it sounded fabulous to me. Working with offenders, in my innocent understanding, would take me one step closer to working with serial killers.

It would be a job share role which again was perfect as I did not want to work full time but my commitment was 100%. I also carried on for one day with my clients at the day centre running a creative group in the afternoon and working one to one with clients the rest of the time. All this was still as a volunteer but it showed my enjoyment of the centre and its service users and how grateful I was to them for adding to my experiences as a new counsellor.

One thing I learned whilst in this role was that the majority of clients that I worked with were genuine people who had experienced a bad start in life and had little chance to escape the pattern of dysfunction in their life. They were streetwise and tough however and there were many times when I felt maybe I was out of my depth when they came into probation under the influence of their substance of choice or maybe just frustrated and in a bad mood. Most offenders were great to work with and like most people are interesting characters. Only on one occasion did I come across dangerous behaviour and that was when I could not allow a high risk offender to see his children that week. His possible understandable reaction was to throw a chair at me across the room. He ended up back in court.

I can honestly say I did all I could for these characters but it became tougher as time went on. Resources were cut and our time working face to face with the offenders was reduced. More paperwork and report writing took over and I felt that the offenders were not being given the time that they needed. The way around this was to refer offenders on to outreach centres for addicts, but again resources were diminishing and there was very little to offer. I was becoming disillusioned. Another factor involved in probation work with drug and alcohol users was that they all tended to live very desperate lives from day to day. Many things went wrong and unfortunately when you are living on a knife edge some of the clients unfortunately died. This became difficult to comprehend and I felt I was no longer able to offer a supportive service that was good enough (this may be my own feelings off inadequacy as I knew I was not there to 'fix' anybody – I could not work miracles!).

All in all it became time to leave. I had time off for stress and after a three month lay off for November, December and January 2007, I started back at probation but my heart was not in it. It is a very difficult job if you are not 100% committed – and I wasn't. I decided to create a CV and hand in my notice.

Whilst working at Probation I managed to get enough hours and experience over the next couple of years to apply for and achieve my accreditation with the British Association of Counsellors and Psychotherapists (BACP). This was a fantastic high for me as it showed that I could do it.

I decided to send my CV to all the schools and doctors surgeries in the area hoping to get lucky. My back up plan was to set up privately and see clients on my own basis in my own premises. I was quite excited about private work and was checking out potential offices that I could use for the work. I had some enquires from a couple of doctor's surgeries and went and had a chat with them about the possibility of working with them.

Out of the blue I received a call from St George's School. I went in for a talk about what I could offer. They were looking for a Counsellor on a part time basis. I was straight away offered a job for three days a week counselling the students in the school. This would be a challenge as it was a big school with a boarding school element existing so there would be a range of cases – something I had not experienced greatly as I had specialised in addictions through my placement and early work. I accepted the offer.

I started at St George's in October 2007 and enjoyed working in a team in the Learning Support Department with very supportive colleagues. I have now moved up to be Head of Emotional Support. The children are great and I really enjoy the freshness of it all after the struggle of probation in the last 12 months. I had landed on my feet and I continue to thrive in the environment of the school.

Chapter 17

Life continued . . . somehow. Hour after hour, day after day, week after week – more of the same old stuff. I kept a brief diary to record what was going on for me, in an attempt to make sense of everything (something I have yet to do). 2005 was a fairly typical year for me, but was also a breakthrough as I avoided any lengthy mental inpatient stays in hospital – the first year for a long time that this had been achieved. Life was not fun by any stretch of the imagination but I was becoming more hardened to it. I expected little.

As I had been suffering from back and leg pain for such a long time and had also been fainting on a fairly regular basis I became quite desperate. A friend of ours read in a daily newspaper about Jerry Lewis, the comedian. He had also suffered from back pain and had surgical procedures that had failed, and like me was at his wits end. In America he had met a surgeon that performed a process called neurostimulation. In this procedure an electrical neurotransmitter is fitted into your spine at the appropriate level and then a wire leads from the implant to another implanted battery lower in your abdomen. It is all under the skin and a remote control is used to turn the stimulation of the damaged nerve in your back higher or lower. What you feel is a tingly sensation of varying strengths which covers most of the pain you were getting before. On reading this article I decided it as worth a try.

It probably is the best time to explain all at once all my operations and the inserting of various batteries over the last few years.

So, via a pain management doctor I was using at the time, I managed to get a referral to the Royal London Hospital in Whitechapel to see if I was a good candidate for the procedure.

After an initial visit it was decided by the consultant and his team that I would be a good candidate so the wheel started to turn, trying to get funding for the procedure on the NHS. This procedure is quite expensive and is not performed privately.

They explained that the neurostimulator they would put in my back would somehow override the nerve damage in my back so instead of feeling pain in my leg I would feel a pins and needles sensation. This would be a considerable improvement on what I had been suffering for years.

It took about six months to get the funding from the Local Primary Care Trust. The cost of having this done is many thousands of pounds.

I was constantly checking with the consultant as to when it might happen and to be honest my belief was fading in the whole thing, when after about 9 months the magic call came. I received a letter inviting me to come to the hospital at the beginning of August 2005. I phoned the hospital of the designated morning as requested just to check they still had a bed for me which had not been filled by some emergency and at 3pm got a call to say come now.

The underground line from Kings Cross to Whitechapel was closed following the recent spate of bombings we were late. We had to take a different route in, not really a problem but the train seemed to stop everywhere. Just as we were boarding the train we heard rumours of bombs in London.

At about 20 minutes from the hospital I got a call asking how far away we were. I thought we were late so I said 15 minutes. The receptionist said to continue on our way as we were so close but with the bomb warnings the hospital was on red alert and only emergencies were being admitted (and now me). We arrived soon after and were let in after bag and body searches.

The surgery was the next day and I was the first on the list, which is great as you do not have to worry waiting the next day.

The night before was eventful. Hospitals are always noisy places at night. The girl in the next bay to me, who had recently had a brain tumour operation, tried to climb out of the window of the fourth floor ward as she had had enough. Unfortunately the window was next to my bed so I got a ringside seat. She was eventually calmed and we all went back to sleep.

The anaesthetist and the surgeons came early the next morning and at last I was in the operating suite waiting to be put to sleep. I had no nerves as I always think of the anaesthetic as the first step to recovery. When I wake up I am just going to get better.

The procedure involved 8 days in hospital. Firstly they would take a small amount of bone from my spine around the level of my bra. Then they attached a small neurostimulating implant to the nerve that they had identified as being problematic. They fed a wire out of my back near to the wound. This way after the surgery had settled down and all sensations in my abdomen and legs were normal they could attach a battery externally to the wires to check that all was working.

The operation of putting the electrode implant in my spine was a success. A day later I went back into surgery to have the wire implanted under the skin, running from mid back down to the front left of my abdomen where the battery was implanted under the skin..

Four days later they connected a battery up to the wires coming out of my body. Immediately I felt stimulation and after they had set the channels and the frequencies I had huge pain relief. The final stage of the operation to put the battery in my body would be done in two days time. They would put the battery in my abdomen and implant the connecting wires from the electrode in my upper spine to my lower left side abdomen in my front.

This was a success and I left the hospital two days later with the feeling of being bionic as I had a hand held remote control to change and manage the frequencies and I had a relatively pain fee leg for the first time in many years.

The battery that was implanted was supposed to last 3 to 5 years. Things never go to plan!!!

In March 2007 I experienced a disappointing sensation - or lack of it. The battery had died. I went back to the Royal London and they confirmed, by connecting me up to their computer, that the battery was dead and would have to be replaced.

Back to getting funding approved from the local Primary Care Trust once again.

Changing the battery could be done by local anaesthetic but I faced a wait for funding and then available bed. It took about 3 months and a great deal of suffering from the pain. Eventually this was done and once again was great. This time the battery only lasted 1 year and I was back again at the hospital. The doctors decided that the answer was to insert a rechargeable battery, a relatively new invention from the battery manufacturers but something that could solve my problem.

My problem was that I had to have the battery on 24 hours a day and a high level to stop the pain. This gave me great relief but was draining the battery too quickly.

I have to say that the funding came through very quickly and for that I am eternally grateful. For the operation they had to open my back and fit a connector to the electrode in my spine, rewire down to a new battery site just above my left buttock and remove and close up the old battery position. Afterwards I looked and felt as if I had been through the wars and travelling home that night on the train felt awful but there was no leg pain. There were now three wound sites where the old battery had been removed from, also from the new site of the battery, and also from where the new connector had to be fitted to the original stimulator in my upper back.

Recovery was okay although one of the three scars became infected before healing properly.

A success, thank goodness. This has lasted to date. I have to recharge the battery every couple of days. I have a device like a phone charger that powers a plate. I then take the plate and hold it over the battery in my body for about an hour in order to recharge the battery. Relief I hope for a long time to come.

After the first operation I felt great but like all things the euphoria fades and I sank back into the everyday depressing world (or so I thought) that I was living in. The physical pain was minimised which helped enormously but the anxiety never left me and the hallucinations were as vivid as ever.

Chapter 18

Thurs 15 December 2005

10pm in bed tired. I am feeling anxious about tomorrow and work, getting up early and facing the world. I am staying with Mum this evening feels comfortable and safe. Excited about Ed, and family coming but feel lost without T, Olive and Roxy.

Fri 16 December 2005

11.35am Probation Office (*this was my place of work where I was employed to counsel offenders with drug and alcohol issues*). Felt isolated and unsafe so felt I needed a break and phoned T and Mandy (*a friend*). Put ipod on and had a musical distraction.

Later I feel a reason for being here and feel wanted albeit with expectations. Feel like I need to put on a front or fall down. Staying this evening with Anna.

3am (Anna's house – *another friend from counselling training days*) Wishing I could have said no. I enjoyed the evening but cannot relax into it. I am always looking for the next thing to happen. Excited about going home, afraid of being in a strange house.

Sat 17 December 2005

6.30pm at home

Relaxed although have the feeling that I need to go out. Concerns over eating in front of people – why? Don't want to drink – how can I say no?

Positive and happy.

Monday 19 December 2005

At Probation 9.30am. Excited as have three new clients today but frustrated as again the IT and computers do not work. Felt isolated and I do not want anyone to 'break into my place'. There are loud voices in my head, but not scared. I am looking ahead again and need to remind myself to stay in the day. NOW!

11.45am. I am impatient – difficult to sit and wait. Restless 30 more minutes to wait before a client. Had a biscuit – disappointed in self - planning not to eat lunch although I know I will feel better this afternoon if I do.

3.30pm. Anxious and crying. I rang T in order to try to get out of the situation. I am scared of being in the Probation office alone. Worried about setting the alarms off etc. I am not in the moment. Isolating and staying in fear – can others see it? I hope not.

Weds 21 Dec 2005

7.30pm. Restless, anxious, planning – wishing time away and annoyed with self for that. Want to cry but need not to cry now. Must be happy.

Thurs 22 Dec 2005

6pm Driving home from Vale House (*the drug and alcohol agency that employed me to be based at probation*) I cried – all false energy to get through the day and now do not have to = release – I do not know what the feeling is? Loneliness and isolation.

Friday 23 Dec 2005

At work

I discovered that my client of 12 weeks has been charged with 6 counts of rape. First feeling is of sadness then of anger at being deceived, then disloyal – who do I believe?

11.15 bored but excited at going to see James and Nicholas, (grandsons of T) and then Ed, B, & Stella later. Impatient, waiting and feel quite destructive – difficult to sit with self.

Saturday 24 Dec 2005

11pm – Newton Pub (*The village that my brothers and I were brought up in, and where our parents still live today*)

With Ed and Bridget. Excited, relaxed, then tearful and sad – did not want it to end. Thinking ahead again.

Sun 25 Dec 2005

12 noon – Xmas day, excited to see T. Very happy, but for some reason not comfortable, tense and anxiety ridden. Felt very quiet as there was too much noise with all the family there. I wanted to be part of it but kept isolating self which was very difficult. No confidence in big groups – what will they think of me?

2am – more relaxed – lots to drink – planning to go to the gym.

Mon 26 Dec 2005

Left mums – very sad to leave Ed, B and Stella and cried in the car on the way home.

6pm at Mike Hudson's (*A friend of ours who usually entertains T and me on Boxing Day*). Was quite relaxed and it seemed a relief to feel good.

Tues 27 Dec 2005

At home – lay in. Great to be in familiar space with T, Olive and Roxy. Good day. Very 'high' after a blitz at the gym.

Thursday 29 Dec 2005

Vale House – happy! Back to routine.

Friday 30 Dec 2005

Probation 8am – relaxed, back in a safe and comfortable atmosphere where I know what I am doing. Looking forward to going to the gym & swimming tomorrow – impatient.

Stay in the day.

3pm Probation – good, confident, at ease.

Saturday 31 Dec 2005

Party

Nervous, being watched, needing to escape.

10pm – fainted, embarrassed and ashamed. Why can't I be like everyone else? Wanting to cry. (*I tended to faint when I could not cope with everything that was going on in my brain and also sometimes if I was in busy or stressful environments. New Years Eve was not particularly unusual as it was at a friend's house, but being sociable all evening felt a bit daunting!*)

New Years Day – 1 Jan 2006
1pm – still in bed crying. Low, feel ashamed about last night.

4 Jan 2006
Home alone! 8am–paranoid and scared walking around the house.

Tues 10 Jan 2006
8pm at home alone as T is in hospital for a knee surgery procedure. Fear of people watching. Had late call to work but told them I could not do it! Made excuse then felt a failure. Where is my commitment? Why haven't I written for so long? Disappointed at 'giving up'. Avoidance do not really like looking at how I feel. Started smoking again.

Sun 15 Jan 2006
Home 7pm – about to go to Mandys – impatient. Half pleased and half displeased that swam half mile in 16 minutes which was good for me, but my body knows it now. This is something I told myself I would stop doing.

Friday 27 Jan 2006
At home after Bolton week. (*Bolton week was a week where T worked at a junior tennis event that I went to help out with*) Pleased to be home – new idea. I am anxious about all the things that I have to do. Pleased to be planning again – looking forward to mid march Thailand trip. Keep in the day – out of the question. Why? What feelings?

Sun 29 Jan 2006

At home 7pm. Been swimming feel high and excited that I can still push myself if I choose to. I am slightly disappointed that I had to prove to myself that I could – knackered shoulder. Difficult to write but looking forward to pilates tomorrow and already planning next swim distance and times etc feels quite desperate. (*This obsessive pattern of behaviour is often a perfect deviation from experiencing and focussing on uncomfortable feelings for me*)

Tues 31 Jan 2006

8pm at home – This is the 3rd day in a row when I have been happy. – I have energy without restlessness, ability to relax and take things on. New client at home – nervous – sense of achievement at gym. Motivation to keep living. Warm happy excited and looking forwards.

Weds 8 Feb 2006

8pm home. Excited about Hong Kong trip booking. Looking forward, really difficult to stay in the day.

Restless. Tired after swimming but satisfied. Planning to exercise more.

Fri 10 Feb 2006

At work 12 noon. Felt guilty about writing family stuff for Annie

She asked me to describe my family. Will show Annie but no one else. In a way I felt as if I was moaning about my lot. Felt quite emotional writing about family but also a bit liberated. Today am still aware of feelings being close to the surface.

Fri Feb 24 2006

8.30am at work. Tired. Anxious but feel it is very important not to tell anyone. Planning the end of the day – swimming blitz – who cares about shoulder and neck injury – need to get thinner through more aerobic exercise. It could happen.

Weds 22 March 2006

3pm Probation. Tired but pleased with day. Back at work after 2 weeks holiday visiting family in Thailand. Busy with sense of purpose, also see it as a new start as started a new exercise programme and am back on a diet to get in better shape. Increased aerobic exercise and core stability and fewer weights. Feel highly motivated and excited although tired through jet lag. Feelings = motivated, excited, useful, busy, distracted from same old shit, impatient – want to go to gym now.

Mon 27 March 2006

11.50am Probation. Feeling physically tired after two hard workouts at the gym over the weekend and pilates this morning. Realise that I like this feeling that I have pushed myself even though I am struggling with concentration and the voices telling me to give up. Restless and keen to push myself further – will do this by not eating anything except tomatoes. Waiting for work to get busy so that I can submerge myself in that. What am I running away from?

Weds 29 March 2006

Driving home from supervision felt grown up and confident. (*When actually doing things on my own and coping I tended to get this 'grown up' feeling that I could do things independently*)

Thurs 30 March 2006

At work leading a group on Transactional analysis. Still cannot believe that I have this job. Responsibility and grown up feelings.

Friday 31 March 2006

Probation – conference. Feel grown up and a good feeling to be learning. At a friends for dinner. Vulnerable and did not fit in - no real reason for this feeling except the usual difficulty of being around people.

Sat April 1 2006

Relaxed, nice sunny day. Felt safe.

Work out at gym – felt great and tired. Feeling of being in control and happy.

Relaxed but excited and still planning ahead all the time. Difficult to stay in the moment.

Mon 3 April 2006

Swam before work and felt good for the day. Busy and buzzy. Left work at 7pm - still sunny felt as if I could run and I don't have to ask anyone. It is OK to do what I want to - free no restrictions and grown up.

Weds 5 April 2006

4pm driving to work. Although being alone has provided the most feelings of being grown up, being alone is also the most fearful state – who knows who is following, panic, voices exacerbating feelings of uncertainty and vulnerability. I hate this even to recall the journey - my journey

Sat / Sun 8 / 9 April
Glasgow Davis Cup – where the GB men's tennis team were competing against Serbia's equivalent team. Crowds of noisy people – petrified. Scared of people behind me. Felt panic rising, very vulnerable. Having to put on a face to mix with tennis officials. Difficult.

Mon 10 April 2006
Probation

Really busy due to next Friday being a bank holiday – fitting people in today. Very voicy and distracted. Felt completely undermined by this when I am usually confident when I am busy at work. This made it worse. Tearful. Cannot wait until Tuesday – day off – Lazy?? Not grown up today.

Weds 12 April 2006
After Davis Cup weekend have felt very stressed and not back to 'normal'. Too much from the voice, twitchy feel vulnerable and uncomfortable. Feel as if I always wearing a mask and not being able to let people know who I am and what I feel. Ashamed of my own fear. Not grown up at all want to self destruct.

Sunday 23 April 2006.
London Marathon Day. Big motivation to get out and do something. Suffering from flu but been keen to get back into the gym. Excited. Going to Cambridge for lunch – hope it goes OK. Feel as if I am the peacemaker even though there is no question that it will not be peaceful. Feel OK can't put a word to it. Tired but kind of excited.

Monday 24 April 2006

Feel shit. Tired, headache, eaten a chocolate. Overrun at work - usually good as it diverts the mind away from voices – today = all too much. Need to run.

Tues 25 April 2006

Visit to Dr R and Annie

Felt good being there. Started to talk about unfamiliar things and external/internal feelings and experiences.

INSIDE OR OUTSIDE?

Upon reading a book one evening, a challenge in itself with concentration being a real struggle with Arthur talking all the time, I read that the voice(s) that one hears are generated from inside your own head. I had heard this before but not paid much attention to it as I could not comprehend that it was reality – it was easy to blank it out. Why would it come from inside? I spoke to T to try to get clarification that the book was in fact wrong, and that my perception of an external voice was in fact the truth. T explained to me – in his words – that part of my brain was in fact generating the voice of Arthur from within me but also making me perceive that it was coming from outside. This was also what I experienced this morning talking to Dr R. He said the same thing. I was mortified about what he was telling me. My mind went blank. Then ideas came flooding in. What bad thing have I done to have my own control centre act against me? How could it come from me when Arthur is a male voice and my brain is all female. I have, in my belief, no way possible of creating a male voice.

T and the book must be in error. It is coming from the outside. Then I dawned upon the answer, radio masts and telephone satellites. These make voices travel and move about without being seen visually so maybe a nearby mast or satellite is erroneously sending me a male voice to haunt me? It would ring true with what Arthur says in that I have done some really bad things in my life and deserve persecution. Maybe this is what is happening with the radio masts and satellites? Peace of mind at last until I revealed my inspiration to T who patiently set about dismantling my theory saying that the radio / telephone signals had nothing to do with my mind as they apparently do not know if I exist or not. I had an answer – helicopters. Many helicopters fly over our house looking for me (T says I am not that important) but if they had been sent by the radio waves to check me out it would all slot into place. Wouldn't it? T disagreed. Tears began as I obviously did not understand anything at all. They were not tears of 'poor me' but tears of frustration at a total lack of comprehension of what is going on in my world and the world of others. T says that if I can work this out I will be on the way to eluding Arthur. I wish but have no belief to follow! Arthur backs up my theory that I get it because I am fundamentally a bad person. Bad people deserve to be hurt, so if I don't hurt myself (which nowadays I largely manage to do although plenty of temptation comes my way nearly every day) someone else may hurt me for him. And now I am getting lost again. Some body help me? I don't know how I can survive this chaos in my head? This episode happened at 10 pm last night and today at work I have been so stressed I have felt right near the edge of my ability to hold on in public. I am still here!!

Felt as if I was deformed or broken – very upset to realise that there is something wrong inside me. Saw Annie afterwards and calmed down. Reduced my suicidal feelings. Feeling very ungrown up! Need to identify when it is my projection that people think I am not good enough or is it my own internal perception. Check it out with people – am I really not good enough? Felt knackered for the rest of the day. Am I good enough or is it just my perception that I am not in other people's eyes? Ask the question.

Friday 28 April 2006

Tired, still recovering from Tuesdays session with Dr R. Disappointed in myself for being so affected – check out other people's opinions but too ashamed to speak out. My self esteem and self worth are very low at the moment.

However I am excited about the weekend – Lion King in London and book shopping on Sunday. Bank Holiday Monday so no work = relief.

4 May 2006

Vale House. Felt good when I arrived but fainted at 10.30am and felt shit all day after that. Have never really got over the appointment with Dr R and that is two weeks ago. Stressed although felt I was dealing well with things. Totally scared and surprised by fainting.

My Body is a Pill Bottle?

32 and getting older! 2006 has been up and down for me as far as the voice is concerned. I started the year with a dodgy January and February which is nothing out of the

usual. I managed to get myself a bit better by the end of February, and with the blessing of the shrink, I managed to cut out the mood stabilizer which seemed to me to be a huge step forwards. Could it last?

No.

By May I was fainting again at work and feeling really stressed and under pressure from Arthur who was relentless in his need to break me. A doubling up of the Stelazine (usually the most successful anti psychotic drug prescribed to me) was hopefully going to do the trick.
It Didn't

Back on the phone to the shrink who recommended some time off work so I took one month. During this time he also cut out the Stelazine totally from my drug regime and replaced it with quite a high dose of Chlorpromazine – an old and fairly sedative drug. For the first two days I was on another planet hardly managing to stay awake for any length of time, and if I was awake I am not quite sure whether I was connected or switched on! It did have the effect of helping to reduce the impact of Arthur and to relieve the constant anxiety that I experience. A week in Eastbourne was on the cards for a tennis tournament in the capacity of a spectator. This would be the venue for the next minor hiccup on the drugs front.

The sun was shining in Eastbourne and after a day in the sun my skin was burning like a furnace. I had tried to keep out of direct sunshine as it was very hot but do like to get a tan to feed my vanity. The new tablets did have an extra warning on the say so of my shrink and also an extra label on the bottle from the pharmacy to stay out of sunlight – I was just beginning to experience why. My skin on my face and arms was scorching like little pins being stuck in and out and very itchy. This was day one. As the week progressed I became a bit of a hermit hiding under layers of clothing and a ludicrous pink floral hat donated by my Mum but was actually very useful for covering my head and ears! After a week of cold showers to relieve the irritation and pain I rang the shrink again who confirmed all was Ok and true to the British weather the sun went in and rain saved the day for me. The skin problem appeared to be solved – the end of my problems?

No.

With some of the older drugs side effects tend to be more marked (in my experience). With the mood stabiliser, Sodium Valproate, that I periodically take throughout the year I always feel that I put on weight. This drug had been reintroduced to my cocktail prior to Eastbourne alongside the Chlorpromazine and the two drugs together are currently helping to turn me into the world's largest lady! I may joke about it but it is not a great feeling which also piles itself on top of the already mountainous troubles I feel myself experiencing at this time.

Earlier I had outlined how it was to be in control of food and body image – imagine how it feels now with this control seemingly rested from my hands. I cannot totally blame the meds as I am sure the powers of self discipline required to maintain a low weight and good figure have been lacking in recent months when other problems centring around Arthur have taken precedence. On writing this piece however I am still in the mind set that I am on day 2 of my latest diet and have been to the gym twice in two days. I have to restart my counting from the beginning as my path is not as direct as it used to be and I branch off to take time to watch a movie or go out to dinner or espresso and almond croissant with mum at Prêt a Manger! The intentions are still virtuous and strong; the action needs to be improved to gain results.

This all leads back to that obsessive problem where I become immersed in an ambition and drive myself to that end with no notice taken of any possible stumbling blocks, for example if I say I am to run for half an hour today I need to do that despite having a sore ankle that needs a day to ease off. Old behaviour rears its head again. The addict never dies! (I don't know whether to admit this but I am quite glad – I like the addict in me at times – it is a good way to get things done!).

Chapter 19

Tennis was no longer a solace as the glass box, which had previously allowed me to hold it together whilst playing in front of people, had been violated. For as long as I can recall on the tennis court I imagined myself living in a glass box where I could see out at people watching but could not hear them in return. Everything was mute as if listening through a window. This provided the isolation I needed to perform. Once this isolation had been violated it has never been the same again. Not one moment of peace anymore. The voice within became a constant torment, and trying to deal with it is also very hard work.

Because it is so stressful living under a death threat I have taken on board many different ideas to ease my discomfort. One suggestion provided by Dr R, my psychiatrist at the time, was to listen to music. This may seem straight forward, and music was something that I had used in the past to manipulate or to raise my mood. One special thing about this suggestion was that the music should only be listened through headphones so that it is just you and the music. Then to add to this suggestion was the idea that you should listen through just one ear, and that would have a much more beneficial effect. I was sceptical but tried it – to my amazement one headphone in my right ear was much more effective in reducing the intrusiveness of the voice than listening through both ears at once. Because of this breakthrough music has become a big part of my coping mechanism inventory for dealing with everyday voices. I can be alone without the worry of being watched whilst music channels my energies into a positive mood rather than the abject fear of reality.

The type of music I listen to is varied. High energy 80's music can lift my energy levels, but also Nick Cave and Morrissey do a good job of spreading their form of gloom so I can relax in the knowledge that I am not alone in a world coloured in black and grey. Classical music or music without words can also help as it is the feel of the music and not the mountain of words that bombarded my brain along with the usual voice. That soothes away from me the libretto of life. Just melody and feelings help to create a space in my mind to relax. Sometimes when listening through my right ear I can accompany this with a visualisation in my mind of a positive place. I have a particular that I like to revisit, in my mind, which is the Negev Desert in Israel. I once went on a sunset camel trek out into the desert. No one there apart from our camels and silence. Golden.

Another coping mechanism suggested by Dr R was to learn a foreign language via listening and repeating which has possibilities, in his experience, of helping those who are taunted by hearing voices. I tried. I got stressed listening to the Italian voices to repeat in conjunction with my head voice, questioning what I was doing. Arthur was not silenced and it just became frustrating. I even tried learning the language to music but that was a step too far.

Another avenue for escape has always been exercise, literally running away from the problem. With the neurostimulator fitted I could return to some sort of exercise which had in the past helped my mental state.

Exercise has been part of my life since I started to play tennis at school aged 8 years old. At this time I had no awareness of any ability let alone belief in myself.

I dreaded school sports with the exception of after school tennis or badminton, for which I represented a local club and used to be vaguely successful.

As tennis took over physical activity became more central in my life, although off court training was still an anathema to me; and I still had no joy or belief in the value of running or sprinting around cones or other seemingly meaningless tasks that regularly took place.

When I was 11 years old, I was in a tennis squad with players who were 14 or 15. My playing ability meant that I could hold my own on court, however at the end of each training session we would all hit the streets of Cambridge for a run. One evening I tripped and fell on the way up the road and when I got back on my feet the trailing people had disappeared around a corner, and I was lost on the streets waiting to be rescued. When they got back to base they realised I was not with them and they retraced their steps until they found me.

My confidence was low before that but now it was lower than low.

I do not how , when or why things changed but at sixth form college in Cambridge, I used to get an early bus from home in the morning and go running around the school field followed by a jump rope routine all before lessons. I felt good. The buzz was there and that has become a familiar friend in more recent years.

Swimming was popular with me as it was a non impact sport and was likely to safe for my back even in its decrepit state. As I began to swim regularly I would get more competitive and try to swim further and faster each day. The rhythm of the swimming and the breathing meant that I could relax in a state that was calm and pleasurable. The sensation of being underwater meant that my experience of the voice was minimised. It was like being in the glass box and all I focused on was the beating of my heart and the concentrated effort to go further and faster. A release. Not only a buzz from the exercise but also the treat of it happening in a world of almost silence for me. Tranquillity. It was a time when I was alone and also after exercising hard in the water it left me feeling completely spent and empty which a relief after any of the complex emotions that I exist with in a normal day.

At the risk of sounding like a right fruitcake I am going to try to describe another couple of facets of my life that keep me busy . . .

Another worry in my confusing existence is that of counting words or spelling words out in my mind. This happens especially whilst walking upstairs or on a pavement where the cracks provide hidden dangers.

If I have to go up or downstairs or happen to be walking on a pavement with cracks or lines on, or a patterned carpet I grasp onto in my mind the last sentence or words that I have spoken or thought about and either spell the phrase out letter by letter or word by word with each precisely placed footstep! This takes a lot of concentration but is also second nature so there is no escape. If the stairs come to an end and the phrase matches the correct number of stairs or steps on a pavement then my mind can rest at ease (until the next time) and I will stop counting and spelling. However, if I do not finish on a round word or phrase then the counting goes on until I have piece of mind that ends with a suitable place to stop ie when the pavement stops, the next flight of stairs, a change in colour of the carpet etc. If I do not get to finish my counting then I am in a state of panic that I have unfinished business and will often go out of my way to get it finished in my mind. Quite exhausting especially if I get it to work (it always does in the end) and then I have the incentive to seek this feeling of satisfaction again. Some people call this obsessive but to me it is daily life.

I also have a problem with being alone and it takes unusual forms.

When T goes out to meetings in the evening I usually stay with a friend. On this particular evening my friends were all out so I chose to stay at home alone. It was only going to be a couple of hours. I can do that. It was fine at first but then about an hour into being alone I started to feel afraid. I phoned Annie, I was lying on the sofa with the phone next to me. I hardly ever call Annie between appointments and I think she was as surprised as I was ut it was okay. She suggested that I try to do something to distract myself from the fear that engulfed me. Her suggestion was to cook dinner for T when he got home, so that I would be busy until he got back. After talking for ten minutes Annie had to go. I was back alone with my tears. I could not move. There was no hope of me making dinner, I could not move to put the light on, or talk to the dogs – my usual comfort blanket; and certainly could not venture into another room. I just lay there in the dark silence. I was frozen.

It has also happened to me whilst in the bath and in a swimming pool.

I run the bath looking forward to a long hot soak and all is fine. Then I get in and am sitting in the bath before lying down and get frozen in the moment. Fear. I want to lie down but cannot bring myself to do it. I just sit there with my head on my knees scrunched up to my chest. I cannot stretch out or relax but just sit there frozen sometimes for as long as twenty minutes. I eventually can get out of the bath and go to bed. In bed I can lie still and it will not be noticed. I feel safer not moving.

It happened in a swimming pool in Thailand when I was visiting Steve and his family. We were in Hua Hin and I got up at 5-30am and went for a walk along the beach. It was beautiful; the beach was quite busy as the locals tend to go out early before the searing heat of the day. I walked for about an hour and then returned to the hotel pool for a swim. I got into my swimming costume and slid into the water to a level where I could stand just with my head above the water. The water was succulent and cool and perfect for a swim following my walk along the beach. The place was silent. I stood rooted to the spot and stood and stood. For an hour or so I stood rooted to the spot not able to move an arm or a leg and frozen with fear. I do not know what enabled me to move after an hour but eventually I managed to get out of the pool. My trip to Thailand alone had been such a challenge and each hurdle I had flown over no problem and now this. I went swimming with Steve and the kids later in the week but would only stay in the shallow end. I could not test myself in public.

These moments of fear come over me at the least predictable moments but I am hoping that the more time I spend alone the more I will be able to cope. I need to break the pattern as patterns form the basis of my behaviours and I do not want this to become one. If I try to do something and fail it comes back to haunt me.

In another moment of fear was when I decided to jump in front of the 11.23 train from Harpenden to London. I almost never go on trains alone because of the fear that I might jump. On this particular day I was going to visit B and Stella and decided to catch the 11.23 train. I got to the station, bought a ticket and as I was going across the bridge to the platform the train pulled in. I was too late.

I got on the train there was no question of me waiting for another. Maybe I did it on purpose as I an unlikely to act on the urge but it is enough for me to worry about it.

One random negative impulse, one negative comment from Arthur at the wrong time and there are too many factors rushing around in my brain for me to trust myself.

Another daily 'hang up' of life being scared is the dreaded telephone.

When I answer it my immediate worry before picking up is that I won't want to speak to the caller or worse still they won't want to speak to me so have to wriggle around with a load of bloody small talk before palming you off to get the person they really wanted to talk to – waste of time in my mind. Another problem is that I may not recognise the voice on the other end of the phone that rabbits away ten to the dozen and I have not got a clue whom it is. I finish the call no wiser, in fact more confused, than I was before I deigned to answer the phone. These problems can largely be minimised with mobiles and phones that now throw up names and numbers of the caller so I can be selective about whom I choose to talk to – power to the receiver!?

The other side though is more of a worry. Me phoning others. With the exception of a few (which I could count on one hand although the list is beginning to grow) calling people creates a major ordeal in my mind. I have friends who when I have been round at their home drinking wine and chatting the phone rings and after much cursing it is answered begrudgingly. I generally assume that people I call have busy lives and fall into that category of 'oh god it's the bloody phone again. . .' therefore when I make a call to them I have this picture in my head of the well practiced scene of cursing the phone before politely answering. For this reason I do not want to be the inconvenience of their day or evening encroaching into their all important time. I am getting better however at calling folk especially people I do not know as I cannot as clearly picture their blaspheming.

The evolution of email and the internet have given me a perfect escape route to solitude and silence if I so choose. Some people love to talk to on the phone and get a great sense of belonging, if I feel at ease calling someone – it can only mean that I feel accepted in their lives and worthwhile talking to.

Just a thought, just a quirk!!

Chapter 20

My moods are influenced by many factors but one quite significant pattern was that my moods dropped at certain times of the year. November was always difficult as was January and February each winter. I was reassured to know that this pattern is not uncommon, and Ed also has dips in moods at similar points in the calendar.

The troublesome winter of 2006/7 saw a dip in my experiences so significant that Dr R suggested ECT again. This time it would be as an outpatient at the Priory twice a week for three weeks. This meant travelling to Roehampton on Tuesdays and Fridays for a 7am start. Dr R convinced me that techniques and technology had advanced since my previous experience of ECT at the Wellington under Dr L. My memory should not be affected as much, which was a big relief although I did not really believe him.

I was off work at Probation for the whole of December whilst I was having the ECT.

Back to where I never thought I would be again!

This time at Roehampton Priory as an outpatient which makes the whole thing more faceable. The insurance company will not foot the bill as I have had this treatment before so it is coming out of my husband's pocket which makes it even more important to me that it works. It has not all been plain sailing – My shrink tried to arrange it for me on the NHS but came up against brick wall after brick wall as far as communication with the right people was concerned. Then I needed a blood test and chest x-ray to take into the Priory on my first visit. These were done via my GP who is unpredictable to say the least. The x-ray had to be done privately in order to get the films back in time for my planned initial ECT and the blood tests were done at the local hospital and the GP suggested that the results would be ready in time for me to go and collect them for the first ECT session. This did in fact work but took numerous phone calls and much stress – just what you need.

The first session I was told that I had to be there for 7.30am which meant leaving home at 6am with dogs in tow!! It was the quickest run through to Roehampton ever and we were there by 7am. After waiting for 45 minutes the ECT nurse rescued me and explained the procedure. This was reassuring as she had previously been a nurse on my ward when I was an inpatient in past times. I had to answer various basic questions for the anaesthetists and a consent form for Dr R. I was reassured but so nervous. There seemed to be endless people when I wanted to see as few as possible. Arthur was taunting me telling me not to speak to the nurses, not to co-operate, don't trust the man who puts you to sleep. I have won if you go to sleep as you will never see life again etc. But I did it.

I do not recall waking up or how I got to my cell on the ward where I was brought a black tea which I must have requested, apparently I turned down any breakfast which does not surprise me as my recollection of Priory food was desperate at best. I remember being asked if I could remember T's mobile number to call him and tell him all is OK. I got it wrong the first time but when the nurse came back to help me remember it was all OK. I remember coming home and sleeping most of the day with a splitting headache, but little else has stuck in my mind.

This however is miraculous compared to previous experiences of ECT where I had no recall of anything, anybody or where I was on coming round. I hope to keep this up through out the course. The nurse explained that they had 'zapped' the right side of my brain only which affects my non dominant left side and should have less deleterious effect on my memory – so far, so good!! As far as benefits from the first session I cannot be certain. I have slept well since and not woken in the night so frequently which is a blessing but my body has felt like it has been through a boxing match with very sore neck and shoulders. This has reduced over the next day or so.

I will attempt to record my experiences and feelings as the ECT progresses for interest and my own benefit to see my journey. Next stop Tuesday 5 December 8am!!!!

ECT 2

6th December 2006. The day after ECT 2!

The morning after was good, but after a broken nights sleep I felt OK. I was feeling quite lively and hyper and in a positive frame of mind which is new and the good energy seems to come without hangover or side effects from the ECT. Relief. As the day progressed I began to have the fear of the voices again as Arthur became more dominant and controlling - I felt the need to run and escape. I became quite tired and paranoid as Mum and John kept asking me if I was alright as I didn't look 'as if I was with them' whatever that meant! I kept fighting though and feel that I did as well as I could have done today. I didn't cut myself although desperate feelings to do so, but John noticed the small cuts on my wrist and the inquisition followed as to how I had done it, to which I lied adeptly I hope. Worrying now about tomorrow but have a more solid feeling about coping at the moment. Desperate for another positive day – cannot spend my life being a failure.

ECT 3

08/12/06 – day three today.

Nervous after one good day after last ECT, and then having one low day. Nervous about review with Dr R not knowing what he was expecting or how successful ECT 1 & 2 had been in his mind. I was open and told him that I felt I had achieved one really good day and then one bad day again which he felt was very positive and lifted my hopes again. It is good that a reaction of the positive sort has occurred even though it hasn't been sustained at these early stages. Also reported feeling hyper after the treatment which, again he was pleased with.

ECT 3 was uneventful. I went in at 9am and woke up at 9.30am pulling the tube out of my throat which was quickly rectified by a nurse on duty – they are always surprised by how quickly I come round! After a couple of cups of tea 1 hour later I was on my way home complete with customary head like a hammer and jelly legs! Chatted to another patient having ECT who had had ten weeks of bi-weekly ECT and is now having weekly sessions – I don't think my head (or T's bank balance) could cope! She seemed OK so who knows her story?

Overall a good day. Slept at home for a few hours and now out to the theatre in London tonight to see Cabaret (booked prior to knowing the ECT dates) I hope I won't sleep through it all and my head will cope. Back to the straight and narrow tomorrow – roll on Tuesday and ECT 4!

ECT 4

Tuesday 12 December 8.30am.

A restless night in anticipation of another early morning. I do not think that I will ever be able to sleep deeply if I have an early appointment the next day. The traffic was good and we arrived in good time. Everything was routine – I am getting to know all the ECT staff now they are great. The same process – stickers on head to monitor the ECT then the anaesthetic which is the best bit when the room goes wavy then dead. Then next thing I can remember after today's ECT is being with Dean the therapist in Garden Wing lounge being given a cup of tea with milk in it – fowl!!! I must have been a bit woozy as I would never have asked for this if I had any sense about me. Crashed out in the lounge with a headache for an hour and then T and Teresa came to see me and to let me go. Teresa (head ECT nurse) is really pleased with how the ECT is working and even suggested that when I see Dr R on Friday before the treatment he may suggest that I do not need the last one. I would however like to finish the course as I feel I have been getting more and more cumulative benefit as the course has gone on.

The drive home seemed quite long as I felt quite nauseous and had a splitting headache despite a handful of paracetamol before leaving the Priory. Once home the usual routine of sleeping and a light lunch and now full of life with a slight nauseous feeling still pervading but happy to be bouncy again (much to T's horror!!!).

Roll on Friday for the next instalment. Still no real side effects which is great and much better than I could ever have hoped for. Hooray!!!

ECT 5

Friday 15 December 2006

Friday 6am trip to the Priory – getting to be a habit! Feel quite relaxed now that I know the routine. Am going to meet Dr R before the ECT today for an update as to how it is progressing and how many more I need. For some reason a bit nervous about this – the ECT has made me feel so much better it is a bit worrying that I will lose that if I stop the ECT. How long will it last – I know it is just the negative part of me taking over again but I need to beat it somehow.

Dr R was late. Everything was fine though and we decided to do today's ECT and then ring in on Monday morning to see how I am before Tuesday and the next date for ECT. This was fine by me.

The ECT went according to routine and I was leaving the hospital by 10.15am with the usual crashing headache but apart from that feeling OK. The usual couple of hours kip at home will solve that – it will have to as I am off out tonight with some friends for a Xmas celebration, and then tomorrow off to Paris on Eurostar for lunch at George V for a surprise birthday party. Nothing like giving myself a chance to recover.

Arthur is still kicking about but not so intrusively and I do not feel as controlled by him which means I can relax a bit more. I don't want ECT on Tuesday and after discussing it with T we decided it would be more beneficial to try to get back to normal over Xmas week especially as I am hoping to return to work next week. I have been summoned to a meeting with my managers regarding this and this is the next sticking point in my recovery as I am worrying intently about going in and having to explain things.

I rang Dr R and he agreed that it was OK not to go ahead with ECT 6 and I would ring him the week after Xmas to check in with a need for an appointment either straight away or at the end of January. I think I need to get my medication sorted out as I am still taking a lot and not quite as good as I was a year ago back on the Stelazine. That can be my challenge for 2007.

ECT has exceeded my expectations as I now feel I can function on my own without putting myself at risk. I have energy and restless feet which is new again and is OK by me but drives T insane – perfect partners!! I now know that ECT can change the pattern without huge side effects which I do get from the Chlorpromazine (especially in the sun) which will become a problem the closer to the summer I get – it seems a long way off but when med changes take a block of weeks to take effect time soon passes. Overall happy for Christmas – lets keep going.

December 19th – last ECT – felt high – looking forwards to Xmas, back to Cambridge, family, need to get out and about shut in – enjoyed being with family but inside there was a tension trying to shout and run off. I wanted to go back to work on Dec 28 after six weeks off, but was told to get note from GP to sign me back on. My GP failed to do so – he refused as he did not feel that I was well enough. In a state of displeasure I went to Dr R – he refused also and suggested one more month off which I agreed to reluctantly as I must have had a level of trust in Dr R. So I took January off work and went swimming and to the gym a lot. Picked up energy and motivation and felt much better. I was glad I didn't rush back to work in December. Teen Tennis (the Bolton Week tennis event mentioned earlier) was a good week where I felt independent and able to look after myself. I kept away from the tennis a lot but got involved when I wanted to and it turned out to be a good week. I was looking forwards to going back to work on Feb 5th still high with energy and motivation.

I was edging through January tentatively finding my feet when one morning I woke up and there were a group of men surrounding the bed – very real not ghost like angels, I thought if I laid still and did not move they may not know that I was there – what the hell were they doing there anyway? How was I going to get up if I was surrounded by men? After 30 minutes I made the effort to open my eyes and look again. The coast was clear so I rushed out of the bedroom and started the day. Adrenaline rush from a close shave. Is Arthur stepping up his campaign to cripple my confidence completely? I tried to think no more of it until, of course, the next day. Again the sombre ring surrounded my bed but as I moved they backed off – Arthur is not so strong after all – is it just a scare tactic, had I become complacent about him and his existence? I spoke to T about the ring of men and he laughed heartily and suggested that it was not possible. He tried to convince me that if anyone had been in the house the dogs would have gone berserk. I laughed with him but could not convey the real fear they instil in me when I wake up in the morning. He suggested I walked around the room with my arms outstretched to waft away the traces of anyone being there. Who does he think I am? Would you be ready to stand up and shove men out of the way just to prove a point? I have never done it and now (early March) the figures are there some mornings, just as daunting, and some mornings I awake to peace. Work started first day boring as just sorting out diary and paperwork. My first client the next day was very aggressive and confrontational. I thought 'what am I doing in this job?'

On the Sunday prior to going back to work I met a close colleague who asked me if I had thought about getting alternative employment. I had been thinking but no definitive ideas. Then my accreditation application was accepted bringing new motivation. This made my counselling qualification to be of a higher validation which was really positive. Clients picked up and got better – lots of no shows but time to get back into working ways.

February 25th crap day. Felt as if I couldn't go on – just wanted to cry all day – felt self destructive thoughts of cutting self again but need to stay good for T and other people in my life that don't want to live with a miserable old cow. Trying to lose weight – another stress what if weight doesn't go down – becoming an all consuming issue. It was becoming difficult to explain to people how I feel. I woke up one morning and felt low and uncommunicative, just wanting to shout and cry unable to keep the tension inside, energy low and no motivation. Told B when she rang that I didn't know how to deal with it all. Want to come off Chlorpromazine prior to our holiday to the USA in April but am now questioning as to whether I will be able to do this. Also questioning as to whether I can really do this job that I think I love but seem to get very stressed all the same. Work goes on, a large number of clients have not been turning up – is that me or am I just being unlucky at the moment. I am spending the majority of my time doing assessments as this is where the process starts – eventually they will come back to me after the court hearing and sentencing to alcohol treatment. I can't wait to get stuck into some good continuous work week after week. I have just been asked to assess a prolific very high risk sex offender where I need to go to a hospital to assess him as he is currently sectioned. I said I would do it as saying 'no' is something I do not do easily and I do believe that all offenders should be given the chance of appropriate sentencing and follow up work. Mixed feelings that I am looking forward to the challenge and excitement of a high risk offender and doubts as I do not like sex offenders and also can I handle the pressure that goes with it. I am still feeling very fragile at work and on the edge of coping despite the lack of client work. I can't run away and have to be present and available. Why can't I be happy? What scares me is the thought that I can't do a *'proper'* job. I can't imagine being able to work full time and in a rewarding job which requires input I seem to struggle. Practice makes perfect, apparently, so I will just have to keep at it and try to support myself rather than sabotage myself every time I feel the heat.

Chapter 21

The year 2008 must have progressed smoothly after the winter of 2006 /7 and my last blast of ECT.

I had been looking forward to my step brothers wedding in Tasmania and the trip was somewhat something of a breakthrough as I achieved a lot on my own (even though travelling with Mum and John). It did however take a lot to enjoy such achievements.

The trip to Australia and Thailand was one had really been looking forward to. I loved both countries on previous visits, and I would get to see Steve, Ding and the girls.

We had three days in Bangkok on the way to Australia. The girls, Gwen and Maggie, had both grown up so much and had more confidence around people, which made interaction and communication really fantastic.

I shared a bed with Gwen and a friendship was formed that I really treasure. I had to put my fears to one side and reassure Gwen in a hotel room without Maggie or her parents (they all sleep in the same room at home) that all was OK. I loved the responsibility which made me feel grown up and normal-but internally the strain was building.

Onto Australia and Tasmania. Tasmania was a quiet place but with many changing faces, from small towns to rainforests, to beautiful secluded beaches. We hired a car which I drove for most of the time for the nine days exploration of the island. Of course the wedding took place and Chris and Kats family and friends were there, but I think I coped OK. I could not afford to fall apart at this stage – it was not my time. I did not want people to worry about me when the focus should be on the happy couple.

After Tasmania we had three rainy days in Melbourne which were great, with the highlight for me being a trip up the Great Coast Road. We spent fourteen hours on a bus but the scenery was wild and fantastic, and the characters on the bus kept Mum and I amused.

After Melbourne we moved onto Sydney and the weather was beautiful. We stayed in an area called The Rocks which is close to where we stayed for the Davis Cup. Chris and Kat were there so we spent evenings with them and found a great secluded spot at Watson's Bay to while away the days. Quite relaxing – even for me.

Back to Thailand for five days, where we went to the coast at Hua Hin with Steve and the family. It is great there with plenty to do and night markets to explore for bargains. The Thai food was beautiful and the company relaxed. I felt I had to be responsible with Gwen and Maggie as they attached themselves to me which I loved but at times felt worried that I could not do 'it'. I do not know what I had to 'do', but my default setting is failure and that is never far from my mind.

The trip back home was long but not too stressful. I do not like travelling on a plane as I do not feel safe from possible attack. On arriving home – April 8 2008, it was thick snow!! Nothing in my life is predictable.

April 15, 2008

I have been back from Australia and Thailand for one whole week now. The jet lag is conquered but the residual tiredness from a long haul holiday and a week back at work still lingers. I was glad to be home from the holiday with my Mum and John that I did enjoy but also missed T greatly. Although I thought I could and intended to, talk to Mum and John as much as possible and to let them know how I was feeling, it was a different story when it came to practice. I tried to tell them with a two day time delay on how I was feeling, ie I would say, I was having a bad day a couple of days ago but would

always end it saying but I am alright now. The trip was fantastic and the only thing I would have changed about it was for T to have been able to come.

Back home for a week and back at work but today is Sunday so day off. I only work Monday to Wednesday, at the moment, in a relatively new job that I basically enjoy as a counsellor in a school for 11-17 year olds. This is quite refreshing after the stresses of probation and the addicts.

The school is fairly high achieving which brings its own problems and there is also a boarding element to the school so kids often need someone to talk to. It is generally a good place to be but quite demanding and often hectic, which I find somewhat stressful. I like going in to school, but it is quite a large establishment with about 1400 students. Being scared in crowded places is not a good characteristic to suffer from in a busy school, yet that is the environment in which I find myself.

Also the feeling that I have a timetable that I must stick to regardless, and the feeling that I am trapped there from 8am to 4pm without having the luxury that I had in my previous job where I could just pop out for five minutes to get some space. Everyone is there to fulfil their potential and I need to be an example. It is for these reasons that I savour my time off and dread Sunday evenings when I know it is nearly over.

On this given Sunday, my husband and I, had been invited to a charity lunch hosted at some palatial home. We were invited by some good friends with whom I am more that happy to spend my time with. Unfortunately I knew not one other person at the lunch and had to sit making polite small talk with people who all seemed out to impress. The place was packed and therefore scary for me who can't deal with people sitting behind me for the fear that they can 'get to me' without me being able to keep an eye on everyone to check I am going to be safe. I had a few drinks to get by on – I thought that it might help me to relax, but also leaves me with the feeling that I am taking risks so the anxiety courses through my body. At the end I was the happiest person to leave, with T a willing accomplice.

I survived the bash but now it was Sunday evening. This signals the end of my free space. I started to get panicky in my mind and went to have a bath and to go to bed to just get over the feelings of fear. In fact I got so stressed in bed that I started to cry and went to seek T's company. I tried to explain to him the feeling that I had no comprehension of how I was going to get through the week ahead let alone the night I had to endure first. Nights are always the worst time if I wake up at all. I had this feeling of being totally overwhelmed and incapable of dealing with the voices and the anxiety that either causes or results from the voice that I hear – it is kind of a chicken and egg puzzle, which came first?

Eventually I succumbed to sleep and was totally exhausted. I was to wake up to Monday feeling as if I had been trampled all over. It is a physical feeling as well as psychological. Why is that?

Chapter 22

Monday 14 April 2008

After last nights fears and distress I rang my psychiatrist to get an appointment with him this Friday which has given me something to focus on. I am seeing my therapist on Thursday and my psychiatrist on Friday so if I can just reach that stage of the week I think I will be doing well. School happened. It was busy as exams are looming and kids and staff are under pressure to meet deadlines and targets. This does not directly affect me but I see the fall out when kids are not meeting their expectations or are afraid of failing and not getting grades to act as an entrance to the next stage of their education. The counselling is particularly busy which has taken me by surprise a little as often the beginning of term starts a bit more slowly and business builds up as the term progresses and everyone gets tired and fragile. The only good thing about this term so far is the fact that British Summertime has started so school finishes with a light evening to enjoy after the school day. I found very little worse than finishing school and going home in the gloom to a cold, dark evening inside. I am very much a person who needs outdoor living and exposure to fresh air. Walking the dogs with T after school is the highlight of my day!!

Tuesday 15 April 2008

Life at school is getting to me. Demands are flying about left, right and centre and it seems to me like everyone wants a part of me. It is hard to believe the different types of problems the children at school have. Arthur, the voice, is getting me down telling me that different people in the school are watching me and planning an attack. I need to keep my eyes peeled to prevent such an attack and also if I am walking around the school I take circuitous routes that no one would be able to predict and therefore stage an attack. I am determined to be one step ahead. I guess that is one bonus of having Arthur – he does provide a warning that people are about to attack me or are they?

Wednesday 16 April 2008

Only one day to go until I see my therapist. This is my last working day of the week – hooray. Or so I thought. One last trauma with a seriously anorexic pupil with whom I am working meant that I have to come into school on Thursday morning to see her before an exam. I only live around the corner so I justify this trip into school before my day really kicks in is no problem. Deep down I resent this eating into my freedom. I do not resent the pupil in any way at all, in fact I will be happy to work with her but part of me feels my boundaries between work and home blurring just because my boss knows that I live just around the corner and can 'pop in' for a special reason.

Thursday 17 April 2008

School again but only for an hour. Today's challenge is different. I have an appointment with my therapist in

London and have to brave the trains and underground system to get there. It has become a thing that I like to do on my own to stretch myself out of the comfort of being escorted everywhere and to maintain some semblance of independence. I have been working with my therapist for a number of years and feel totally comfortable with her and her rooms.

The train was on time and the tube was not too busy. I felt knackered and desperate for a coffee to wake me up and thought I would have time when I got near to my therapists rooms. I had a ten minute walk down Sloane Street to my destination and I usually enjoy this walk as it is fresh air and open space after the intimidating tube ride. However sometimes I feel the threat of open space. I will have no cover if someone decides to attack. Today Arthur knew this and was talking incessantly about men on the street who wanted to kill me. I suddenly felt quite dizzy and was spurred on to get to the therapy rooms and to get an espresso and to have a cigarette to calm down. This was a usual routine on my therapy days! I went on and had thirty minutes to wait which did not bother me as I thought I could just get myself together – which I did. When I was collected by my therapist to go to her room I was following her then all of a sudden I was on the floor in a heap with people around me. I had fainted and people seemed to be around me asking questions – 'what happened? did you faint?, have you had anything to eat? Has this happened before? Etc. It has happened before a number of times so I wasn't afraid of the faint, I was petrified of the people around me – who the hell are they? Are they the people Arthur has been warning me about? Shit there is too much to think about. They took me into the therapy room and this man took my blood pressure and laid me down on the couch where I spent the rest of the session.

The session was strange with it being suggested that I was trying to do too much and needed to manage my time better, especially at work, and needed to give my self some space and care. I find this difficult to take on board as many people work much harder than me and do not have to bail out at the first scent of stress. I guess I feel like I have failed again.

I was due to visit Ed & B & Stella after my session and stay with them over night which is something I look forward to from one visit to the next. My therapist and a doctor at her rooms would not let me hit the underground on my own in my state so booked me a car to take me to B's place of work. I agreed reluctantly. I didn't know B's address but could roughly describe nearby buildings. Despite this I ended up in the wrong location and had to ring B to find out where I was. Another cab ride later and I was safely ensconced at B's with another life saving espresso! I felt totally drained with a banging headache and Arthur shouting abusive messages at me about being near people and how I was going to die that night. I really didn't care.

Friday 18 April 2008

I returned by train from Ed & B's early this morning so that T could take me to the psychiatrists. Dr R, for once was on time and we spoke for about an hour about how things were going and my moods being particularly low and the voices and symptoms being difficult to deal with. Before my trip away he was thinking of putting me on injections of medication to see if my body could absorb them differently and achieve a different effect if this method was used. There was no mention of this on this occasion, but he wanted me to try an MAOI anti depressant, Tranylcipromine, instead of the cocktail I am on at present to try to raise my mood which hopefully in turn would help to reduce other symptoms. It will be at least two weeks before I can start as I have to reduce other pills first. This type of medication is new to me and it comes with a condition that I cannot eat certain food types whilst taking these pills. Cheese is the major food I am not allowed to eat. This didn't bother me the slightest as cheese is something that I do eat but realise it has many calories that I could well do without – another good excuse to diet! If I did eat cheese and took the meds the possibility is one of a stroke which the psychiatrist went to great lengths to explain to me would not kill me but just leave me paralysed – so don't even think of it. Sometimes it really annoys and frustrates me that people can read my mind. Whose side is he on???

Saturday 20 April 2008

I woke early worried about catching a train to London Bridge for a bereavement counselling course. I was hoping for a reasonable sized group so I could merge in and leave early without being noticed such was my attitude on the day. My motivation was fairly low despite enjoying the subject area. When I arrived at the building I found the room with three chairs set out only and the tutor. He asked if we minded continuing the day with such a small group and of course we all said yes despite my misgivings. The day progressed and was interesting and fairly safe as there was only a couple of others involved. It really suits me better with a small group as I can memorise the group members. I know, then, if I see other people in the room they are not real and therefore do not feel intimidated by them. By introducing ourselves to the tutor I knew the other two who existed and anyone else I could see in the room I just had to discount them. I can do this in my mind but still feel threatened by what I perceive as being their physical presence in the room. By a matter of elimination I can confirm to myself that they are not actually real. Sort of! I rushed home after the day on a packed train that was probably the most stressful part of the day as I had no idea who was real or unreal – sometimes I have to give up guessing and just accept that they are all there.

We had four friends coming for dinner which was something I wasn't really looking forward to – just because I felt stressed from the day. I liked all the people coming but didn't feel in a good space to be cheerful all evening. T had prepared some great food and I hit the wine to try to lift my spirits. It went well but I just felt like crying half way through the proceedings but survived to see the end. I kind of splurged on everything that evening and then felt guilty and ashamed all night. How could I have so little self control. Tomorrow will be different.

Monday 21 April 2008

School – I never look forward to school on a Monday morning. The week seems an interminable endurance and I can never see a way through it – many demands unknown but as yet I haven't failed to do my job so this bothers me again – why do I get so negative about it?

The day was long, or so it seemed, but passed eventually. I do have a good friend there who makes the day a bit lighter.

We were due to go out with good friends which I had been looking forward to but felt knackered on returning home from work and not really motivated to be sociable and chatty. However when I got there the evening was great. I decided about a week ago that I was going to stop drinking as I was clutching at straws at something that would make me feel better. However when I go out I feel I need something to get me through the evening and immediately turn for a glass of red – no problem. I did have a couple of drinks but nothing too extravagant and felt OK.

The day had passed and I had survived. Roll on tomorrow.

Tuesday 22 April 2008

The morning came around far too soon. School was a nightmare for no recognisable reason only that I was very tearful in the morning and had to keep disappearing in order to cry in private. Sometimes crying is all that I can do for relief. I just felt sad and scared. Sad – I don't know why; and scared of the voice that kept telling me I was going to get shot by one of the students in the school. The afternoon was better not being as tearful but very down and very quiet.

Over lunchtime three separate people questioned me as to why I was so distant and not speaking or joining in. I just said I was tired but it makes me worry as it is really important that people at school do not know about me and my fears. My boss knows vaguely about my diagnosis but nothing real about how I function, or not, day to day. The day ended and I cried all the way home. I can't walk into the house crying so I have to stop at the top of the road to get myself together – I feel so useless and feeble but it just overwhelms me. Today is the second day without taking citalopram (an antidepressant). I am blaming the withdrawals for why I feel so bad.

I had arranged to go out in the evening with a friend to the swimming pool. I did not want to go but knew that I should as I cannot give everything up – the fight goes on. The evening was ok and I am glad that I went. I just dreaded the next day making a pact with myself that I was going to go in late. Sometimes it is easier to blame the fact that I am tired rather than to look for any other reasons.

Wednesday 23 April 2008

Again I felt very low but was more determined to hold it together and not to let anyone notice. For this reason, when the alarm went off I felt that I had to get up and go on time. The day was uneventful despite being bombarded with kids who have far more problems than they deserve – it focuses the mind and makes me stronger in resolve to keep going. That lasts for about 5 minutes and then I am back to my own world. The day passed and home was a relief – nearly time to relax. I had a new client at home, who I was reluctant to see as I did not feel that I was in the best space to take on more work, on the other hand it feels good to be wanted. I saw her. It was a very positive experience and I enjoyed it. I felt that I understood what I was doing and was comfortable with it – not a usual feeling.

The day ended then and relief was overwhelming – enough to make me feel tearful again. Some sort of yo-yo.

Monday 28 April 2008

I started on 25mg of Amitryptiline last night to supposedly help me sleep ie to do the same job as the Mirtazepine that I was taking but had to stop in order to start on a new regime of meds in the next couple of weeks that may help to control the depressive side of my problems a bit more effectively. I slept fitfully and resented having to take the Amitryptiline which for some reason I have 'anti' feelings against. I know not the reason for these feelings as I have used the drug several years ago and cannot recall any negative, or in fact any experience of the drug at all.

I went into work at the school as usual. Full of trepidation on a Monday morning not understanding how the week will pass without something sinister happening to me. When I get stressed sometimes it shows in me, and on this Monday morning I showed my true colours and fainted in the corridor at school. Luckily there were not too many people about and those that were there didn't panic and scraped me off into a quiet room to recover. I hit my head on the floor in falling which added to the headache that I suffer after such a display. I was adamant that as few a people as possible should know as it could be the beginning of questions about my health being asked which I cannot cope with. Also the embarrassment at not being able to cope – the reason that in my mind seems most likely to cause the faint, is something that I would prefer not to be widely known.

I went home to my next night of Amitryptiline induced sleep which failed again to take hold and a night of tossing and turning rounded off my day nicely.

Tuesday 29 April 2008
I got up feeling awful. I was very tearful with a splitting headache and a very light headed feeling. I went to

school and had a quiet day timetabled which I was grateful for and shut myself away for most of that day not daring to walk too far in case I threw myself to the floor again in a bid to make my body understand that my mind cannot cope. The school day passed.

On returning home I had an email from a private client that I see suggesting that she came tonight. I felt immediately that I couldn't do her justice and set about contacting her to change the date. I left messages and emails but did not actually make contact so could not rest assured that she had been diverted temporarily until after the allotted time that I half expected her to arrive. I like seeing private clients as they bring something different to the young clients that I see in the school counselling rooms. This variation keeps me fresh and motivated in what I do, but I need to do it on my terms.

The evening progressed and we were due out to dinner with some friends which I could probably do without but I knew when I got there I would just switch on to auto pilot and be sociable letting the men talk about golf and just chipping in to show I was there really. It was OK.

It was a day to double the Amitryptiline at night which again had no real impact on my sleep or lack of it. This always happens during a period of change in my meds.

Wednesday 30 April 2008

I had a better day at school, probably knowing that it was the last day of the week for me before jetting off to Sardinia for the long bank holiday weekend. I made it through the day but arrived home in floods of tears which signalled a release at the end of a difficult week for me on the emotional front.

I had arranged for Dad and Pat to come over to dinner (not exactly at home but at the nearby Italian!) as it is his birthday tomorrow. This was OK and I enjoyed it but did not manage to eat so much as I was quite nervous that everything went OK. When I look back I do not know what there was that could go wrong but at the time there is always concern.

As we are travelling tomorrow the dogs had to go into kennels for the weekend. Olive does not mind as she is a gregarious and sociable, but Roxy is a home lover and I always worry about her. When my mind is in a state of stress there are smaller factors such as the welfare of my dogs prey on my mind to worry me further.

Thursday 1 May 2008
It was an early 3am start but this was OK as I was excited to be going away. Going away always seems to be a solution in my mind despite being afraid of the unknown and unpredictable. It is kind of like clutching at straws I think. Anything that breaks the negativity of everyday life is good.

We arrived in Sardinia to a nice hotel in small but busy town on a public holiday. The narrow streets trap me but overall it was a better day. I enjoyed 9.30pm when I switched off for the day after our early start and finally got some sleep.

Friday 2 May 2008
We decide to drive around the island today to find some-where to hang out and relax. Arthur, my accompanying voice, was very prevalent today and I felt like crying all day but didn't want to give in. We drove for most of the day and when we eventually made it back to the hotel the

relief was palpable. Even when I know it doesn't matter, I feel a responsibility to direct T who was driving and I get very stressed within myself. I would hate for him to know that I find it so difficult, but I guess it is just another facet of me that I am not comfortable with.

How do people relax?

Saturday 3 May 2008

Crap day from 5am onwards. Arthur started early with suggestions that there were snakes on the balcony trying to get in and I wanted to wake T to see if he had a gun that I could shoot them with.

I didn't want breakfast as I had no appetite and felt generally low after a bad night. Spent the day wandering around after spending some time relaxing (or trying to) on a quiet beach. We had dinner in the old town and I cried for fear of the people closing in around me. I also needed to know whether the food was prepared freshly or was pre-prepared. I needed to know what my chances of being poisoned were.

In all, it had been an awful day. I felt scared all day with the possible exception of the first 15 minutes on the beach before I felt the sand move and fear that there was a man under the sand trying to get at me from below.

Sunday 4 May 2008

On the beach again most of the day which was great as it feels good to be under the sun with a warm body. Somehow when I am warm I am less tense and cope with Arthur better. When the beach got busier I needed to walk out into the sea which was shallow for some distance, so I could have a wide view of life on the beach and keep track of any potential dangers.

Tuesday 6 May 2008

Back to work. Felt rough all day and fainted again at lunchtime in the corridor of our Learning Support Dept at school. Had been feeling light headed and 'spaced out' all morning and struggled to concentrate with Arthur, the voice, telling me I was about to die and I should let people know I would die in the next few hours. When I did faint then I was scared as I thought that that was it – the end. All those times in the past when I have wished my life away I suddenly realised although I may not be happy I am still hanging in there. Of course people in my department were asking about why I had fainted, had I eaten, did I want a biscuit, get her some water etc. It is so difficult to reassure people that I am fine and will be OK. They do not know about Arthur or the every day stress that I feel I have to try to cope with a professional face on. I had been very busy and felt under pressure to help certain kids who were struggling to keep their heads above the sea of work flooding their way pre exams. There is no place for any weakness on my side and when this builds up I guess I cannot cope at a certain point and faint. I felt such a failure to myself and to those that I am trying to help. I have a fear of it being as regular occurrence (today was the third time at school) and what would I do without my job. I struggle to cope with it but would be lost without it being there. I may complain that I find it difficult but have not been a person to walk away from a challenge.

This evening I had the experience of a new private client which although I worry about I really enjoyed working with. The client was totally different from the sort of situation I am in at school so is always refreshing in one way although tiring in that it is another hour of concentration required. Last night was another night without sleep so I hope tonight and tomorrow will bring better fate.

Wednesday 7 May 2008

There is always cause for celebrations on a Wednesday morning as it is my last day of the week. I have a full day at school and a private client this evening but the end of the week is in sight. I slept a bit better only waking up at 4 am and 5.30 am before being awake at 7 to get ready for work.

I felt better today but Arthur is still threatening me that today will be my last day alive. I can't cope if I listen too much to him so have to really try to continue with life without that distraction. People think I am quiet because of fainting yesterday and being under the weather but unfortunately I know that it is everyday life that I have to deal with the intrusion.

I had one student who was very distressed today but good to work with so I felt I had done something worth while. I have the feeling that I need to work in order to get some positive feedback which doesn't come in many areas of my life. The sun was shining and everyone was in high spirits. Exams start soon and many students are in their last week at school before study leave so the atmosphere is changing from the normal trudge of everyday repetitious school life to excitement and nerves about what is to come in the next few weeks and then the long summer vacation.

Again I expected a private client this evening and I was looking forward to seeing her. On opening my emails on arriving home I found she had child care

problems and had to cancel – my weekend comes early!!
Tomorrow morning is my counselling supervision which
I rely on, but then I am free to do as I please until next
Monday morning when the repetition starts again!

Monday 12 May 2008

Yesterday I started on a new med, as planned, as part of
my ever changing cocktail. This one, however, I was
apprehensive about. In the past when Dr R has prescribed
new meds or changes in the routine of taking certain
prescription drugs I haven't been in the slightest bit
bothered, and more recently haven't cared as I have been
in such a dip I do not really believe there is a way out.

Having fainted at work I was so scared as Arthur had
been telling me all day that it was to be my last day. I
didn't care – what if it was my last day? I was frightened
but not frightened of death – just the immediate threat
of Arthur. Then I passed out, just for an instant, but
enough to go crashing to the floor again – the second
time this week. It was at this time when I thought 'oh my
god, what if this is the end?' I realised I wasn't ready to
die just yet. This should have been positive but I found
it such a fright that I fell apart. I couldn't tell anyone at
work about it as they know nothing of my illness and
I try my hardest to hide any weaknesses or limitations
that I feel may affect my perceived capability at the job
I am doing.

Dr R then prescribed a new MAOI drug, an anti
depressant, but of a different category, with which you
need to maintain strict controls on what you are able to
eat – The main offender being cheese of all sorts, broad

beans and pickled herrings!!! Not too challenging on the surface but there were others that crept in on the list and the consequences of eating one of the substances whilst on the MAOI are increased blood pressure likely to lead to some paralysis or more commonly a stroke. Before if you make a mistake with your meds you have to overdose greatly to cause trouble (tried and failed), or you just omit taking them and feel the symptoms take over again completely with a total lack of grip on reality and fear takes over. If I made a mistake on the new meds a stroke would not kill me and I would have to live an even more depressing life – I didn't think in my own small world that my life could become much more sad and miserable (on better days I reach out of this desperation but recently there have been few of these moments).

I played my first competitive tennis match last night for twelve years. It was with my mother in a team, the other pair we were playing were around 60 years of age. It is a local club and this is the 4th team so no big deal. Just a bit of fun and playing my mother is really great as she really is keen. My mother started playing tennis at the age of 60. She now plays at least 5 times a week.

After overcoming initial nerves I managed to capture the type of freedom that I have only experienced playing tennis successfully or running through fields cross country – neither of which I have done for some time – partly due to lethargy and partly due to sheer lack of motivation feeling down in the dumps full time.

Thursday 10 July 2008
I woke up as usual and felt a bit down, lacking in motivation to get up and do things. I was due to go

and see my therapist at 2.30 and was thinking about that. Usually I look forward to seeing her as it only happens once a month and I usually have a lot to talk about with her.

On this particular morning however, Arthur was especially vociferous and scary. He was telling me repeatedly that this was to be my last day which I started to believe. He said I had to jump under the train and that would solve all my problems, his problems and I would be one less person for people to be concerned about. The time drew closer and I was kind of excited that it was soon to be all over. I said goodbye to my dogs, they are the centre of my life, and T took me to the station. He said he would see me later and I corrected him and said 'I doubt it'. He did not think this was strange however as I go to stay with my brothers family the night after being in London to see my therapist. This is something else that I really enjoy so T did not question my correcting him as he knew where I was going to be.

The next part of the day is kind of inexplicable. Instead of just going and throwing myself under the first train passing I went to buy a ticket for my journey. I had to queue and was a mixture of nervous energy and excitement. Soon it would be all over. I queued for what seemed like an age and then had my ticket. This is where the day started to go wrong. My plan was to jump under the train that I should have been travelling on the 11.23, just a quirk that I was driven towards. Any old train would not do. I ran over the bridge and then saw the train pull in – I had missed my opportunity – I was too late. I did not wait for the next train to arrive to fulfil my need but instead got on the stationary train and started my journey into London. I was devastated but kind of in shock as to how close I had been to ending all my problems. I went to my therapist and just broke down in uncontrollable tears as I explained to her what had happened that day. We talked for nearly 2 hours about what had been going on and how angry I now was. I didn't really understand the anger aspect of my behaviour but we had a long discussion which helped move me past my suicidal feelings. If you feel you have failed at all in your life this is the biggest failure of all – not being able to go.

Since then I have been struggling as I had already got it into my mind that I would no longer be here and now I have to deal with life again! I am kind of glad that I am still here as I have told close people of my plan and realised the effects of my actions would affect many. I saw the psychiatrist to talk it through with him and he was fantastic more or less saying that if I wanted to die I should wait my turn like every body else on the planet!! This made me laugh – the first time since the failed afternoon – I felt I could move forwards again.

Friday 15 August 2008

Physically exhausted – mentally pleased that I can still push myself to those limits. Played tennis – freedom and confidence. Played with Jake and Molly (Rick's children) – innocence – not being judged. Felt as if I belonged or had a place in life. Evening meal – anxious – have eaten too much and do not deserve a meal – failure to keep control – led by others to keep the peace. Went to bed at 10pm – felt lazy and that I had given up on the day.

Monday 18 August 2008

T out early – planned to go running – rainy – went to gym – felt relieved. I was due to meet friend for lunch so had to exercise in the morning to allow myself to eat lunch which I often skip. Met Tessa – v good – she didn't want to eat either so we just drank copious amounts of double espresso. Felt excited that I had a friend – quite comfortable and relaxed. Restless in the evening probably due to 7 espressos.

Tuesday 19 August 2008

Restless, had to run. Woke up at 5.45am planning where to run etc. Went out with T in the morning planning to run in afternoon despite huge pain in right leg and injured left knee. Felt I had to. Ran in afternoon in rain and felt relieved (and knackered). Went to see good friend, David, in evening who told us he needed a lung transplant otherwise he would die. Because of his age they will not do a lung transplant. Tried to stay with him and support him – when left felt hollow, worthless and very upset. I cried at home in private. I went swimming at 7pm with a friend – good release. Exercise seems to be the only thing that is really positive for me at the moment despite feeling that I am doing OK. Is OK what I want? After the news from David felt I had to push myself again in pool. Also had a glass of wine that Dr R had told me not to drink – who cares now anyway?

Wednesday 20 August 2008

Could not sleep – thinking about David – helpless/alone. I am scared by reality of events. Cried when telling Mum – release and felt better. Still not really accepting the finality of the situation but made it real by telling mum. Played tennis – poor concentration, shattered and mentally knackered. But felt good at being outside and being able to push myself through pain in left knee and right leg / foot. Afterwards regretted it a bit as too painful – felt out of control. Had a biscuit and felt horrified at myself for just letting everything go because I feel sad. Very tired physically and emotionally but scared to go to sleep. Feel threatened by Arthur – head hurts. Feel I can't cope. Let's start tomorrow now!

Thursday 21 August 2008
Got up at 4.15am – could not sleep – becoming a recurring pattern. Looking forward to seeing Jake and Molly. In reality I played with the kids feeling disconnected and disappointed with myself. Had lunch with Sue – more relaxed. Returned home – tired. Headache again. Stressful conversation with T about David – more tears but it is out in the open now – I need to be there for T.

Friday 22 August 2008
Early morning again but who cares – at least you burn off more calories when you are awake and out of bed! Researched Xmas trip away, we are planning to go to Madeira, have invited Mum and John – spoke to Mum – keen. John negative – I was really fed up at how selfish he appears to be. Out during most of the day. Long run which was fantastic although knee and leg fucked – who cares anymore? Went out to dinner with Mum and John who said they did want to come with us at Xmas so came home and booked that – relief. Desperate to get it sorted out – no patience with people at the moment – I hope that changes before I go back to school!!! Booked holiday when got home at midnight – price had gone up

during the day, but just booked it! At least I know we are going.

Saturday 23 August 2008

Got up at 6am and put music on headphones + went back to bed until 10am!! Lazy but really good. Body hurts physically but want to run. Compromise with myself and go swimming which is a bit easier on the legs! God what sort of wreck do I sound like? Thinking a lot about David and how T is dealing with it as he does not mention it to me. I will ask him later when we can go and visit him again. Suffering a lot of headaches but reckon it is just because I feel a bit stressed with my body. Voices a bit troublesome but not too directive. Going on a train tomorrow – quite scary.

Sunday 24 August 2008

Woke at 4am but managed to go back to sleep until 8am. T had already gone out to play golf – not back until 1.30pm.

As soon as I woke up I cried and felt the curtain of depression envelope me. I got up and put music on full blast to try to block out the voices – didn't work! Wanted to run but body hurt too much & pouring down with rain. I couldn't even motivate myself for something that I wanted to do! Did some prep work for school and typed up diploma stuff for three hours. Cried intermittently and also took to doing housework as a distraction. This was difficult as fear prevented me from moving to the kitchen. T came home which I was pleased about; then Mum and John came to go to Stella's birthday party with me. I was not really in the mood to talk to them but did speak on the train. The party and

Stella were fantastic as usual but I felt I could not really join in - again frozen to the spot. There was a girl from Ireland that I knew so I spoke to her and her kids 4, 2 and 5 months – freedom and not judged.

Spent next hour photographing the kids playing and enjoying themselves = good excuse not to talk! Felt as if I was in a different world and totally disconnected and alone – is this what I really want?

We went back to Stella's house after the party with Mum, John, Dad & Pat. OK. Felt transparent as if people were tiptoeing around me (except Stella of course who is fabulous) – didn't care. Came home and went to dinner with T to local Italian. OK. Tired and just wanted to be with T to be safe – felt unsafe all day.

Very scared, too scared to react to do anything about it. Too many people watching me and Arthur is talking about me.

End of day, music back on.

Hopefully sleep will come soon.

Thursday 28 August 2008

Woke up at 5.45am – a lot of physical pain due to knackered knee and damaged nerve in my right leg. No chance of getting back to sleep so listened to music on my ipod until 8am.

Went to counselling supervision and talked about my inability to name feelings, and feeling a fraud as a result. We also talked about anger as it is my theme of the moment. Found it to be quite positive.

Played tennis and felt great mentally but physically wrecked with crap left knee and dodgy right leg. It feels good and satisfying to push myself though. Now in bed at 11pm feeling like hell! I do feel more confident about my ability to work as a counsellor after talking to my supervisor and thinking about conversations I have had with Annie.

1100 calories today which isn't too bad considering that I played tennis for two hours.

Have thought a lot about David today, and in particular Janice who I had a long talk with yesterday.

Friday 29 August 2008

Staying the night at Mums, got up at 6.45am with bad pain in my leg due to no battery, went down and drank coffee. Felt frustrated and out of control, and kind of scared that I might have to live with pain again. It is irrational though as I know I have funding for a new battery and just need to wait for a date. Cried. Felt weak for being upset.

Mum got up at 8am and I didn't mention it to her - we actually went out and played tennis with some friends for an hour. My leg hurt but I gained huge enjoyment being outside exercising and playing tennis which is something that I am in total control of. Felt confident for a change. Afterwards knee was crap as well as the constant pain in my other leg. Went to visit Sue, my ex coach, she taught me tennis from the age of eight. She had a hip replacement yesterday and was in a lot of pain – what am I moaning about?

Spoke to B on the phone – really happy to speak to her; feel a bit lazy compared to her manic lifestyle, but she is fantastic (wonder woman). This is something that I aspire to one day ie being able to cope with life pressures and life events.

It took me 2 hours to do the 45minute drive home as the motorway was blocked. I really didn't care, except that I had to keep alternating the leg that I drove with according to which one hurt less at the time. I eventually got home and felt exhausted – why? Slept for a bit then watched Caroline Wozniacki, a Danish tennis player and a friend since she was 12, play tennis on TV at the US Open – she should be an inspiration to many as she has done so well to get to where she is now.

Came to bed to write diary but do not want to go to sleep because I fear waking up and having another day ahead of me. Voices taunt me about my pain saying that it will never go away – just like him. I can't give up – Think of David fighting for his life.

Saturday 30 August 2008

Woke up at 7am – pain – what's new? Absolutely nothing – felt resigned. Put music on headphones and stayed in bed until 9.30am. Starting another day does not fill me with joy. Apprehensive, not sure how to cope with Arthur and the pain.

Went to junior tennis finals at local event and met Tim - a non tennis friend who works at the same place as I do. Enjoyed his company and actually started to relax. Lunch laid on but I didn't eat any, but did have some melon and two strawberries. I hate eating in front of people – it makes me feel greedy and extravagant. I went for a cigarette to chill out.

Charted a match with Tim, his partner Jenny is a tennis coach, and enjoyed the distraction of having to concentrate on the tennis – the standard of which was appalling and the source of much banter. I had the worrying thought that I was that bad when I was their age and people would be slating me behind my back? Sat there being very judgmental and enjoyed it! Came home and felt shattered – I find it very hard to maintain a public persona all day without having any real 'time outs' just to cry or escape. BUT I did it! Feeling = surprise and fear that I might have to let my guard down.

The evening was spent with Martin and Janet & take away Chinese. This was no problem until I realised that one of their grown up son's was joining us to eat. I suddenly felt paranoid and very insecure. I feel that I do not fit into a family environment. It made the difference between us being two couples or a family. Families are very uncomfortable as I feel constantly in the spot light noticed for my withdrawal into myself. The son, Tom, is a great guy who I love a lot and have known for 15 years, but the family closeness is something that I feel very uncomfortable in and around. I am not part of it and don't want to be. It is too dangerous to get close to a bunch of people. I may have to share some of my world which I am ashamed about. Also there is the problem of eating in front of people again. I feel that all eyes are on me thinking 'well she will be fat and undisciplined if she eats that' no self control weakness.

I go though it and am now in bed after getting T to come up with me as we had been out and who knows who could have been up stairs in the time we were out? We were seemingly lucky though and now I am back in bed writing this with music on again. Another day. Full circle.

Tuesday 2 September 2008
First day back at school – had been looking forward to it but today was fairly ambivalent. First meeting was at 8.30am where all staff had to congregate – I began to feel overwhelmed with 'can I cope' feelings and insecurities.

Sheer panic but there is no basis to it. Felt like I needed to run.

There were no kids in school today so I took an opportunity to look around all the new buildings that had been going up all year and now are reality. Had an OK morning not doing much else and settled down a bit.

The afternoon was a lower school teachers meeting in which I had to speak about the counselling facilities we offer the students. All my colleagues were getting nervous about speaking on their areas of expertise, but I didn't seem to care what the others thought about my words. I am sure half of them think that counselling is about having a chat over a cup of tea and a biscuit!

I spoke to my boss about a training day that I am leading and suddenly she asked about my health – oh god – panic again. She wanted to know if the voices that I hear thought she was evil (you don't need a voice to tell you that). I told her that my voice was not discriminatory and yes sometimes it spoke about her but equally at other times it speaks about other folk. Who does she think she is? My feeling is probably anger and shock at her approach.

The day ended and I went for an espresso with two colleagues and felt quite on edge. Socialising is not easy and I felt uncomfortable and out of place. There was no tangible reason for this feeling but it just seemed difficult to relax. Just wanted to go home and shut the door. Eventually I went home and T was not there – panic – I needed him to be there in order to believe that I was alright. The dogs were great, of course, and helped me to relax a bit. I felt knackered but went to the aqua class that I try to attend. It starts at 8.15pm for 45 minutes but my body was hurting too much so it was a real struggle. The good thing is that no one sees tears in the swimming pool as you can just duck under the water! I do not talk to anyone at aqua any way and just made out that it was the chlorine in my eyes.

The end of today – roll on tomorrow – it always arrives doesn't it – feeling despair – how long can I go on like this? Music on, write diary, lie in darkness, fear of voice, eventually I must sleep.

Thursday 4 September 2008

Day off school – day off everything! Mum is away so there is no tennis which was probably a good thing as I feel physically knackered and psychologically unmotivated. Had arranged to swim with Susan at 3.30pm so went out in the morning briefly to buy nothing in particular! After my customary banana for lunch I went to sleep until 2.30pm then prepared for swimming.

Swimming was great – body hurt but it feels great and safe gliding through soft water that just folds around you to keep you safe. I always feel safer when swimming. It is relatively silent if you keep your head down and that is fantastic. Arthur still interferes but I have just about convinced myself that the lifeguards are on my side and are not there to instigate my drowning. I came home though and my body felt awful – popped a load of painkillers and slept for two hours!

I found Mr Ellamushi's (the surgeon who will replace my battery to my pain management system) mobile number so I rang him and left a message for him to call me. I got no response today. I hope he will leave a message on my voicemail at some time as I do not really want to talk to him as I feel I am just one of many that he has to deal with – why should I get priority or draw attention to myself? I don't want to appear 'pushy' when many others have bigger problems. This brings me back to thinking about our friend David who needs a lung transplant to survive. There are problems and problems. I still feel very sad when thinking about David but I do not cry about him any more as I have visited him many times now and have come to terms with his situation (for now anyway!). I will go to visit him again tomorrow after school.

Oh I forgot the charity golf day that was held yesterday that raised about £20,000 for the leukaemia charity that I do the website for. I am friends, through tennis, with Jenny who lost her son, who was 23, through leukaemia. Now Richard's friends still support various sporting events to raise money for leukaemia research at the hospital where Richard was treated. They are a fantastic group of people that really make a difference in funding such necessary research. I need to update the website now with this fantastic news. Sometimes I kind of feel out of my depth with this and a bit of a fraud as I am still very much in the learning stage of developing their web. I feel embarrassed now if they look at it as they now know who I am in person as they have seen me at the golf event. Anonymity suits me much better!

For now the routine is read, music, sleep and hope! School tomorrow, but still no counselling as yet – just more interminable start of year meetings and testing which does not inspire me in the least.

Sunday 7 September 2008

Woke at 6.18am and listened to music until T got up at 8.15. Felt sad as if I was going to cry, but only because of physical pain and worry that I might have to ring Ellamushi again tomorrow which I really do not want to do! – I will get T to do it as usual. Fear of being judged. Arthur finds this amusing and keeps on taunting me at my inability to talk when I should.

Went and did some stuff for work and felt relieved to get it done. Felt knackered and still in a lot of pain - most pain killers do not touch it.

Had a banana for lunch then went swimming despite the pain. Nothing will stop me until I really cannot do it. I swam a mile in 35 minutes (2 minutes slower than my best). Very tired but did consider doing it all again to try to beat my time! I didn't because even I am not that deranged. Came home and walked the dogs - I usually enjoy that but felt quite destructive. I would never hurt them but I hate myself.

Did some work in the afternoon on the bloody child psychology diploma thing which I feel I am not fully committed to so get frustrated when I have to do it. I am only doing it as it is there to do!

Dinner – didn't want to eat as I have put on a pound this week – greedy, disgusting, lack of control.

Gave up on the day really early – hope I will sleep but do not really care.

Monday 8 September 2008

God, yet another day. Some mornings you just wake up wishing you hadn't. I went into school which was quite a good distraction but as it is all admin and planning at the moment it did not do much to lift the spirits. I got through quite a lot of work but who knows what I will do tomorrow?

My mind is all over the place with Arthur telling me that men in general are dangerous. I had to meet with a male member of staff at break time and was petrified in case he was going to stab me in the car park as Arthur had warned me. I got someone else to go to the meeting for me. It is good working in a mini team of three as I have someone who can cover for me if I need to shoot off. They both know me quite well and I hope we can rely on each other. I know we can.

My knee hurts a lot and I am going to see the surgeon about it tomorrow – it is on my mind. Also I am still waiting for a new battery so I have that hanging over me waiting for a date. T spoke to Mr Ellamushi today and asked him about it, he promised he would make it as soon as possible. I believe him. I don't believe the knee man!

I can't wait for the day to end but on the other hand I do not want to go to bed. I hate night times as if I wake up at any time it is really difficult to go back to sleep as Arthur shouts and threatens me that there are people in the house. I trust my dogs to let me know but part of me is left lying there with my mind working overtime. Music helps but it always means I wake up knackered in the morning.

I don't know what to write about today really – I feel like shit but find it difficult to break that down. I kind of feel separate from the world and stuck in my own little box. I can see out but people cannot see in. I do not know if I want to let people in – I get frustrated as others cannot see my predicament but also I do not want people to know that I am not feeling as if I am in the same place as them. I want to go swimming but it is too late and I have missed the lane swimming times. T would go bonkers as I can hardly keep my eyes open but I am aware I put a pound on last week and need to get rid of it. I have been trying to eat less but need to exercise as well – this is another intrusion on my mind at present – the fear of fat.

Friday 12 September 2008

Got up 6am. Read book and wrote notes. Very good book. Felt hungry but loathed to start eating so early in the day so had a coffee and a can of diet coke. Voices were not made any better by the caffeine intake. Sometimes espressos make me feel really lively and happy, but only for an instant, at other times they tip me over the edge of anxiety and I become more sensitive and scared – that is what happened this morning. I think my negativity this morning stems once again from the physical pain I was in following Thursday evening's tennis!

I am getting desperate for a date for my new battery to be fitted and am inpatient waiting to start the cybex programme that the specialist has suggested for my knee. But today I just felt like I couldn't keep going so when Mum got up at 8am, I said I was fine, got dressed and went and played tennis with her for 2 hours (all the time thinking that Annie would be saying that I had a voice to use and you can say no). The pain was bad but I felt good being in the fresh air and kind of doing something that makes me feel confident and relaxed.

Afterwards we went to the garden centre for coffee and I ended up buying loads of plants. I think they are beautiful and help to give me a peaceful pleasure by watching their transition through the seasons. Let's hope they do not die before I get them home!!

I went to see Tomoko, Jake and Molly this afternoon. Great – I love little people that are so perfect in many ways yet to be corrupted by life. They are spontaneous and exuberant in all their moods, conversations and actions.

Came back to Mum's and went for a walk with Mum & John – very good and quite relaxed. Dinner was fish and vegetables (1150 calories today) not too bad for a day not at school and not at home. Put my jeans on and they fell to the floor so I must be doing something right!!

I am quite tired at 10.30pm so have come to bed. I hope I can sleep and relax tonight. I think I will leave my music on all night again – it is very calming and helps counter the voices.

Saturday 13 September 2008

Got up at 6am – drank coffee and read book 'I am David' – good read but I haven't finished it yet. Felt motivated to read and enjoyed it but could not really concentrate for long periods. Loaded the dishwasher instead! Had music on which makes me feel better and more chilled out mentally. Physically, as usual, felt a wreck after consecutive days of playing tennis. It will not stop me from playing again this afternoon. The benefit of physical exercise outdoors and pure enjoyment seems to balance out the pain. I am planning to run on Sunday but sometimes I find myself making excuses as to why not to go. I will win that argument!

I cannot wait to see T again tomorrow and my dogs. He has been away. I have eaten too much today and realise that tomorrow I will have to cut back and definitely run however I am feeling. I have worked too hard to put weight on again and losing weight makes me feel good and gives me a buzz. In control!!! No one can force me to eat or not to exercise. I am physically knackered though and have loads of headaches but will continue. The trouble is that Arthur picks up when my resistance is low. I had a discussion about trains with Mum and John and decided that maybe at the moment travelling by train is not ideal for me at present – why take the risk? T has agreed to take me to see Annie next week and then I will get a cab to B's and I will have to get the train home early on Friday morning as I have to be in Cambridge for 10.30am! I think I can do it but do not know how I will be on the day. Today I am scared about it. Sometimes my thoughts let me down.

I have not done any work on my Child Psychology course this weekend – I will have to work tomorrow as my days need to be more structured. I have to push myself harder. I am too lazy at the moment.

I cannot wait to collect my dogs tomorrow. They always make me smile and help to keep me positive – they need me and love me whatever. I feel that everyone needs that to verify themselves and who they are.

Voices, music, dark, sleep, pain, sleep, I hope. Tomorrow starts in 24 minutes!

Sunday 14 September 2008

Another long day finished. Up at 5.45am with bugger all to do – fed up, cried and generally felt sorry for myself. It was the start of a strange day. I left Mum's at 8.45 so I could come and collect the dogs from the kennels. Olive and Roxy were so pleased to see me it was really uplifting. I felt loved. I stayed in with them for an hour or so to settle them down and then went for a run on a beautiful day. Came back covered in mud but really feeling as if I had achieved something. After I had cooled down and taken a shower I went to Welwyn Garden City for a few bits and pieces. I was OK but panicked and walked around aimlessly for a bit before ringing T on the off chance that he had his phone switched on. I felt better and attacked Waitrose, but was convinced that I was being followed by a woman with others in the store watching the chase. I was glad to be going home.

I sat in the garden and did some work on the laptop, then had a really relaxing sleep in the sun. When I awoke I saw a large tiger walking around the garden. He frightened me at first but then after 30 minutes of being paralysed in my chair for fear of attracting the tiger's attention, I decided he was on my side. Tyson, as I will call him, seemed to have no intent to hurt me so I guess he is one of mine. I hope I see him again although if he is there then I must be in danger as he has come to protect me.

I know Tyson is one of my people as no one else has even blinked twice when he has been about so I am sure that he is mine and mine alone. I believe he is there to protect me – I feel safe when he is around. He is not always present he picks and chooses his times. If and when he appears I am always reassuring myself that I am safe, but why do I need him? I become extra vigilant of my surroundings – physical and human. What I am positive about though is that Tyson would protect me at all costs, and I do not know what I would do without him.

I felt unsafe and very scared of Arthur after this incident where he kept saying that if I had seen the tiger it means I will shortly die. I was pleased when T got home and I was still alive to greet him. I love him so much and miss him when he is away.

I am still alive! I saw a private client at 7pm which was really positive, and then just wanted to grab some dinner and go to bed! Here I am now at 9.30pm Knackered. Mentally it has been a very difficult day and physically I tested myself again.

✳ ✳ ✳

Monday 15 September 2008

School day. Fed up with people at school being inconsistent in their decision making processes, but in the end who cares? I should be able to see some clients tomorrow which cannot come soon enough. I do not think I am cut out for admin all day every day. Enjoyed the company of the other staff but felt very flat and tired. Someone told me I looked slim which made me feel great but then I had a biscuit so felt disgusted with myself. We went to see David and Janice after school and David looked very tired and not too good. I had a chat to Janice in the garden and she is petrified but there is a huge amount being unspoken between the members of the family. Felt quite low after visiting. Overall I feel disappointed with today but I do not really know why? Arthur sucks.

Tuesday 16 September

Really bad night last night – woke up in pain and then was scared of people in the room. There were four men sitting in the corner. The room was silent, I think, although my voice (Arthur) was not. Those men had heard about Tyson and want to kill him for his beautiful skin. They know their only way of getting to kill Tyson is through me and my mind. I could not allow them to inhabit my mind. There is no vacancy available. I stayed awake from 2am when I first saw them until I finally went to sleep at 6.23 (that is the last time I recall looking at the clock).

School was OK. I had some clients and actually felt as if I should be there. It feels free talking and listening to the kids. I saw Tyson come out of the staff room and wondered what he needed to protect me from in there? Why was he in school? What should I be looking out for? He is beautiful but I cannot get close to him – he is after all wild. Maybe I can relate to him being wild – I like that trait.

I felt shattered by the end of school. I came home and walked the dogs with T and found out that our doggy friend 'Big Man' Henry – the English Pointer, had been put to sleep through illness. This was very sad as Henry was one of Olive and our favourite friends. I felt sad but shed no tears – too tired. I thought a lot about David today. After visiting yesterday he was tired and struggling. I could not get this out of my mind – I feel so helpless sometimes (that failure thing again!). I find it difficult to develop close friendships and when I do, like in the instance of David and Janice, it ends up in pain. Maybe I need to put my guard up again and not let people into me? Is this going forwards or taking a step back? Too many bloody questions all the time – why is it all so complicated?

I still have not called B and Ed – feel lazy; guilty, selfish and fragile. If I ring I will acknowledge to myself that things are not all OK despite this bloody façade of competence and drive.

I need to ring Mr Ellamushi again but do not have the confidence. I need also to see Dr R but have not got the memory or inclination to make the call – I am scared to let people know that I need help and support at the moment. Maybe things will seem better after some sleep?

Thursday 18 September 2008

Woke at 5.45am with a splitting headache. I think from drinking sherry last night on top of my medication. I do not think I will do it again but it was a very emotional evening with David and Janice at the Bean Tree restaurant. David was OK but it is difficult to see him struggling having to carry an oxygen cylinder with him wherever he goes. He says that he is not prepared to accept this poor quality of life. Today is a big day for me as I am leading an 'Emotional Support for Pupils' day at school for twenty teachers in the department. I know I can do it and have no questions about that, but I am wary of how the teachers will react. We also have outside speakers (one being my counselling supervisor) which is reassuring so they do not just have to listen to me all day!

The day worked well my boss was full of it and I need to take advantage of her good mood! Maybe ask for a pay rise!? I got through the day knackered and wanted to go for a swim but we went to see Janet and Martin – good friends whom we have not seen for a couple of weeks. It turned out to be good fun – needless to say I did not drink! It is good to see everyone else happy though.

Tyson was at school all day with me on the flat roof outside our Learning Support department windows just lying there. I was sure if others could see him they would have said. He is majestic and I love him. He came to Janet & Martin's and sat just outside the back door – his paws are huge! It helps me to feel safe knowing he is there as I still feel danger for most of the time (80% probably). I am going to see Dr R tomorrow to talk about what I feel is a gradual decline at the moment. It is nothing major but definitely going the wrong way. My physical pain does not help along with my lack of sleep. I need sleep to recover from a day of Arthur and if I do not get it the struggle is harder.

Friday 19 September 2008

Woke at 6am. Really fed up and restless. Listened to music for about 15 minutes and then got up and had a shower which was great. Relaxed a bit but still was tense and 'stressy'. Tried to go back to bed - that lasted 2 minutes and then went into my library room to write diary and to read till 8am. Helped T take the dogs for a walk which was really refreshing, and I felt special with Olive with me. Roxy also seemed so happy so my spirits lifted.

Went to see Dr R because I feel I am slowly losing it again. We spoke for some time and discussed playing tennis and obsessions that may come from trying to compete in teams etc. I said that it was 'all or nothing' so he sided with the nothing option. This left me feeling kind of disappointed and reminded me of the time that one of my back surgeons told me never to play tennis again. I told Dr R about Tyson the tiger and how I felt kind of safe with him around. I then started to cry and could not stop. I could not explain it and I could not look Dr R in the eye. I just stared deep into my coffee that I was holding and cried. I could not remember what meds I was taking when he asked which made me feel quite inadequate (how can I not know what I put inside me four times a day?). Chatted for a bit longer about Tyson and how he appears when I want to hurt myself – he is my protection. More tears. He went to get T and I cried some more and cannot really recall much about the rest of the meeting. Dr R has increased the Amytriptyline to help me sleep at night. Ironically we came home and I slept for an hour – exhausted.

I worked on the computer all afternoon doing child psychology work but I was not really that motivated so went to walk the dogs with T and sat outside a café together to drink espresso to lift the spirits! I have felt down for most of the day though. I just need to keep going for five weeks before our trip to Arizona. That is my main goal as well as eating less, running further and getting a new battery (not necessarily in that order!). Also learning to sleep again and getting my knee fixed. I have a physio appointment tomorrow to start on a cybex programme. I am quite nervous about this having to go into a new environment and explain my background yet again to some one new. Only a six week programme though - I can do it! (I have no choice) I know I have choices but I feel like I am at a dead end. I am going to party like it is 1999 – a fine idea to go to sleep on. Prince to the rescue – god help me!

Saturday 20 September 2008

Woke at 5.45am, went back to sleep at 6.15 – 8.30 – Very good. Got up though and felt very tearful and down. T had gone out for the morning and I just felt that I could not cope. Arthur kept telling me to set light to myself so I dare not have a smoke in case temptation over came me. Went to get dog food – felt independent and in my own 'bubble world' oblivious to the outside world. Then went to physio of which I was very nervous as I did not know what to expect. She was great and said it would be 'bloody hard work' but we would test and balance my leg strength, quads and hamstrings, and in six weeks of hard work should be where I need to be. I love to be challenged and felt I could throw myself into this until I go to the States in 6 weeks time. She tested my legs and found that the imbalance between the two leg strengths was not too varied, but the strength endurance on the left crap knee was very deficient. Tendon in left knee also knackered! I did however feel an end in sight and thought if I worked hard enough which was positive. I left the physio and got out of the car park and burst into tears. I do not know why. I guess I was just back out in the open and was just one small person in a huge frightening world around me. I could not go home as I feel trapped in the house alone with Olive and Roxy. I love them but get so twisted inside I cannot stay. I went to the shops and had a coffee. Met Tessa, a friend from work, by chance and she is great so made me feel much better. I then went home and worked on the charity website where I can always create work if I need to stay distracted. T came home quite early which was a relief. It was hard to smile though. We took the dogs out and I felt a bit of freedom. Followed this by a trip to see Melanie (T's daughter) and family. I felt alright but aggravated for some kind of reason. I love them to bits but today it just was not happening! Went home, watched TV and cried. Felt knackered and came to bed at 9.30pm – I hope I can sleep tonight. I am quite excited as I am going to see Ed, B and Stella tomorrow and we are going by car so I do not have to go on a train. Trains fill me with fear now and on a bad day that fear could end up being a big horror (or a final peace for me) I am not ready for that final disappointment. Good night. Or, just night, anyway.

Sunday 21 September 2008

Early morning 6am but lazed around until 9am and felt rested. Typed up diary and felt subdued. Went to Ed, B, and Stella's house which was fantastic. Stella ran down the road to greet me which made me feel very special and loved. I had a relaxed day and rolled down Parliament Hill with Stella and B. I haven't felt that free for a life time. Came back home and felt tired but happy, we took the dogs out and I can just remember smiling all the way round. Spent the evening chilling but was restless and tense so at 10.20 I went to bed.

Day done.

Monday 22 September 2008

School. Bloody hectic schedule for week two! I thought of what my therapist said about setting 'do-able boundaries' at work and realised I had not done my job very well in terms of managing my work. I did not have 5 minutes off between 8.20am and 2.40pm when I had a free period to do my admin. When the day started it was not too bad as I could do my own job and liaise minimally with the rest of the team. The lunch time group for year 11 girls was great and went better than I could have hoped for. I went into two English lessons apprehensively but they were great too so I relaxed a lot after that. I felt out of my depth talking to a Nigerian student about her tribal differences in the school with other Nigerian students, but feel I coped OK.

Felt exhausted at the end of the day and went to see David and Janice and David seemed in good spirits which was also lifting. He looked a bit 'red' but hopefully just because he had been out in yesterday's sun. Because he cannot get a transplant here because of his age he has decided to go to America to get it done. He has made contact with a hospital there and is all set to go. He is very nervous about his impending trip to the USA for treatment, but this kind of makes it more real. I enjoyed the company and felt 'grown – up' today. I do not know if that is OK or not!

I had a phone call From Mr Ellamushi, the neurosurgeon responsible for the state of my back, saying that he may be able to replace my faulty battery on Wednesday – very excited and nervous although I still have to wait to see if I can get a bed. The theatre for the operation is booked although I still need a bed space. I will ring his clinic early tomorrow morning early – add it to the list! Hopefully I will sleep although am now in a bit of a head spin.

Wednesday 24 September 2008

Woke up at 5am and thought I should be on my way to Whitechapel. Yesterday saw a rainbow of emotions as I was told I was on the theatre list for a new battery but then later in the day having it cancelled – great sadness. It only served me to realise how desperate I am for it. There is a possibility, according to Richard, the surgeon, that Friday maybe on. I never let my phone out of my sight today waiting for the call but none came. Not unduly surprised as Richard said he had an emergency long operation to deal with that would take all of today so he may not be able to call. Tomorrow I will be on the phone about Friday. I doubt whether there will be much sleep tonight. Nerves, excitement, sadness, hope (disappearing fast again). Feel fat again today – must not become complacent. I might just try to read now to lift me out of the dark hole that I find myself lounging in!

Tuesday 30 September 2008

Night time. Felt desolate today. Now lying in bed with right leg nerve pain and left leg knee pain – what does it feel like? Spiky pain in right leg, this is the pain that bothers me the most. I get frustrated because there seems to be no end to it. It is very difficult to lie on my right side because of the sharp spikiness. I cannot get into a position that satisfies my body. Left knee just aches – who cares, just gnawing away deeper and deeper. Physio tomorrow which I do not know if I am looking forward to it or not? I love doing the cybex strength work but my knee has been quite bad since last times effort. I do not necessarily blame this on the physio but I hate going back and complaining! I have little hope if I am honest and maybe this is the problem my 'negative attitude'. How many times have I heard that in my life? My little toe is on fire I think, the end of my damaged nerve seems to be where the pain collects. It streaks down the outside of my leg and gathers in the two smallest toes. I cannot wait until next Friday when I am hopefully getting my new battery which provides instant relief. Pain is boiling hot and icy cold all at the same time. Sometimes my leg feels like there is no 'real' feeling anymore, it has died but is still painful. Then it has hot and vibrant pain within my leg to the little toes. It is like a swollen river coursing down my leg to the escape at the end of my toes. This is where I am now. I have the most chance of sleeping with the leg dead feeling. Good luck and roll on Friday.

The battery replacement happened and all was well again which was fantastic and the rechargeable battery was fitted to prevent the whole process repeating every twelve months when the limited life batteries tended to run out. This year was a breakthrough in this respect.

As far as the knee pain went, a third operation in a period of two years for the cartilage, sorted that out. General wear and tear which just needed 'tidying up' benefited me greatly. Happy days again????.

Chapter 23

One positive thing that has come from my experiences is that I have had huge opportunities to get to know myself and to have a relationship with myself, which although is turbulent, is an encouraging phenomenon.

This initial awakening came from very painful disclosures about areas of my life and my experiences which for so long I had kept locked away, but they came seeping out the cracks in my armour that I could no longer prevail. By accessing help (unwillingly to start) I began another journey that was to blossom into a main area of my life and my strategy for survival.

When I committed to the Counselling qualification, alongside the therapy and support from the team around me I started to ask my own questions about who I really was and what I valued. This experience over a period of three years of night school and weekend workshops equipped me to fight my own battles and to understand more of what needed to be done myself. My therapist Annie was alongside me all the way, and still is. She is a fantastic support and knows me as well as anyone.

In my relationship with my counselling training group I was open and supported in a group situation; with

Annie I was alone with her – what an indulgence! Both experiences complimented each other although some of the group weekends were difficult to understand and stay with as my internal battles struggle with more than one person in the room at a time unless I am very familiar with them. I see visions of people whom I cannot distinguish reality or hallucination but my tactic is to believe in those I know. For example if I was in a group situation where I know some members but not others I would only talk to the people whom I had seen converse with someone I know is real. Also in some environments such as in the therapy room with Annie, I know that she would not let anyone else in during our time so I know to ignore the people who usually sit on the other side of the room. It is these techniques that I have managed to trust that help me to survive life in the real world of others.

I have picked up more of an emotional language both through the counselling training and placement in a drug and alcohol rehab house, and through experiences with Annie and Dr R. These vocabularies have allowed myself to learn to express myself in a more dynamic and accurate manner. No longer do I have to answer 'fine' when asked how I am – I can talk if I choose to. That is the bonus – today I have developed a method of understanding myself so that I have a choice at these sticky junctures in many of my conversations. I am full of words and expressions and am no longer a hollow shell echoing pain. I have the choice to speak. It is still a struggle to do this in practice but life is becoming more complete (and often more confusing) as I take steps towards my goal of being comfortable with myself.

The belief that I could do this was largely brought into practice when I started my placement at the rehab house and drop in. The rehab house was a seven bed house where individuals with addictions such as drugs or alcohol could come to spend time with safe people in safe environment where they could build a healthier lifestyle for themselves. To do this therapy and self discovery are key. In the rehab building there was also a 'drop in' centre for people with similar problems who are maybe still using substances and are maybe not ready for rehab or have relapsed after a period of clean time. This was where I spent most of my time doing one to one counselling or group sessions for the service users. Counselling and therapy came alive for me and it gradually dawned on me that I was actively engaged in a real job with real people that I felt had some credibility and value. Self esteem rose to just above zero – which was an improvement, and so intoxicating that work soon became one of my drugs of choice! It was again all or nothing. That way I can still avoid real thoughts, feelings and emotions if I bury myself in something that seems acceptable. Work in progress!!

The work of being with people who valued me encouraged my personal relationships with others outside of the work environment. It all started with Ed. He seemed genuinely pleased for me that I had now got employment with direction and room for development. Previously he had made it clear that the office work I was doing was not good enough and that I had to get out and find something challenging (as if life was not challenging enough as it is). I knew deep down that I needed to achieve something but did not really know how to go about it. By securing employment I felt as if I had gained some respect from Ed which was something I valued, as I had always had a desire to be worthwhile in his mind. This was a start. Now that I had a foothold in the family through Ed I started speaking more openly with him about other family members. Ed asks questions fairly directly and this opened my eyes to how development of a family unit can be so influenced by the characters involved. By talking to Ed I developed a picture of myself within the family and wanted to get to know it much better. Since university many years ago I feel I walked away from these familial relationships to take my own direction. I did this and ended up isolating myself and pressing self destruct. By communicating initially with Ed and then with Mum life became more meaningful again as these other people really mattered to me but I had not allowed myself to accept this before. The family gradually became a place of peace and the major step came when T and I finally became husband and wife in October 2004. A fantastic day, the best day of my life, with family and friends around T and myself, totally accepting us for who we are. This was a situation which a short while ago I could not picture. Times change and people are resilient so miracles can happen and we can survive.

Throughout these turbulent times of discovery Dr R and Annie have been by my side. In moments of collapse they are both only a phone call away and have always been there for me. By being able to rely on this throughout my experiences has provided a safety net that is only possible with an impartial person. Dr R works a web of medications which are designed to help my symptoms of hallucinations and depressive moods. Frequent changes, as my needs change, are necessary, and at times my instinct is to just walk away and ignore all the pills and tablets. I never do for more than a day and then usually feel so dreadful I resort back to what I really knew was necessary – why make it simple for myself and take straight forward advice from knowledgeable sources.

The key to my survival is trust. I trust more people these days but definitely only a single figure hand full. Trusting me is a fleeting experience as I really do not know how I am going to feel or react each day.

Not all my stressors are emotional. From spinal surgery several times I have been left with physical pain as a backdrop to all my moods and emotions. This has been another challenge in my life but in the last four years has been managed wonderfully by the input of a neurostimulating pain management system controlling sensations in my sciatic nerve and right leg pain. By having the implant and battery inside my body a remote control can manage the stimulation of the nerve to conceal any pain. I just feel a tingling sensation down my leg where the pain once was. If pain is controlled in my life then emotional control is also easier. Although depression is a large part of my life with the voices and visions, if physical pain is added to the cocktail I cannot cope and just shut down. This situation is managed better these days and I can recognise blips on the horizon. My difficulty is still negotiating these blips or at least asking for help before life becomes too black and hazardous again.

People who know me, and have known me through ups and downs often say 'How on earth do you hold down a job?' Recently I was talking to Dad and he asked me if I was still at work in the school counsellor role? I was quite taken aback replying 'Of course I am', He responded with comments along the lines of surprise that they had not ejected me yet and how could I possibly hold down a job when at times I can hardly manage my life? In my eyes it is not like that – I have never questioned my ability to do my job because of my particular illness. I would be the first person to step away if I felt I could not cope with the daily (three days a week) efforts of employment.

In my previous job at probation counselling offenders with drug and alcohol addictions, the stakes seemed to be so much more visible as the clients were so physically as well as emotionally vulnerable and unwell that it became something that you had to deal with if a client had an overdose or fell down stairs drunken and died. I think that because the stress was different there, battling against lack of resources, to help these often young vulnerable people, that I needed a change.

As jobs are not easy to come by I thought I may just set up privately for the time being and give myself a break before launching into my next endeavour whatever that may be! I started to look around for premises to base myself, but also out of interest I forwarded my CV to all local schools and GP surgeries. I was unsure what to expect but out of the blue I was called by one of the local schools, and after a couple of interviews took on the post of School Counsellor at a local secondary school with approximately 1400 students. I have never looked back.

By getting in at the right time at the school I was fortunate to pick up a great job. A huge range of issues making my life varied and self motivating. I help to co-ordinate a small team to look after children with problems from friendships to bereavements, to divorced parents to depression and panic attacks. The form of the counselling is mainly on a one to one basis with me; but as a team we offer and have developed social skills groups for a growing number of kids with Aspergers, and also emotional support groups for young boarders at the school trying to cope, or also year 11 girls (aged 15/16yrs) struggling through adolescence up to GCSE exam time.

I cannot afford to have health weaknesses and I live my life at school with an image of confidence and capability. I buzz around the department helping people out and listening to the children. The staff have totally accepted me and even ask my advice on how to deal with certain students or situations and their respective parents. Counsellors are expected to cope. This is where it helps my survival – I have no choice but to survive or leave. It means too much for me to leave so I must survive.

Generally I have done this well although at times a few cracks appear. I when I have become overloaded with voices, visions, hallucinations, work, stress etc. I tend to faint and fall down. Obviously this is a cause for concern for people I work with, who see me, but recovery is quick and despite a splitting headache I can usually carry on. My excuse to colleagues has been low blood pressure and back pain or something along those lines. To survive I must lead my life carefully.

I also experienced difficulties when I took an anti depressant of the category of MAOI's. This meant that I was unable to eat cheese or alcohol (among other things), at school many of the lunches contain cheese and I often got an inquisition on why I was not eating anything but fruit at lunch. Again I used the blood pressure tablets as an excuse. Obviously alcohol at school was not an issue but for the duration of taking the medication I avoided social gatherings made up of school colleagues and friends.

By putting on this strong capable front at school I amaze myself as to what I can pass myself off as. Underneath I feel a bit of a fraud but again that is my issue to deal with. Success surprises me! I use the five minute car drive home from school as a transition back to the 'underneath me' where if I am worried I can ask or express it to T or just shut down and chill out. Often I will do paperwork when I am at home as TV isn't my thing; but this helps my day go more smoothly as I am usually up to date and organised.

My job is a huge piece of the structure that holds me together. I get a breather approximately every six weeks when there is a school holiday period. I can recharge my batteries and repair any cracks appearing in my façade.

Most of all I enjoy the life and the ongoing challenge of school. Annie had said for a long time that I would find my way working with children. She thought it would be in tennis, but I am now working with these kids in school. I feel comfortable in the therapy room and love the challenges raised on a daily basis.

School provides a challenge in other ways. I hate crowds and feel threatened by a lot of people. At break time and lunch time at school 1400 children hit the corridors to navigate around the site. I have learnt the best times to traverse the school to avoid finding myself in the crowds. But I have done it and am here to tell the story.

My learning is ongoing, and by facing challenges it becomes more complete. Survival for me is largely about facing my demons head on and proving to myself that I can do it.

I am not the same as other people. I do not believe that I experience the same existence as those around me. I feel quite removed from everyday life in many ways, yet rely on those around me to provide reference points for me to hang on to.

When talking to Annie I realised that I do not understand the world as others see it. I feel a barrier around me and my experiences as if they are separate to every day living. By keeping them separate I keep myself contained and safe. I am controllable.

Instead of relaxing and enjoying the company of others, they first have to pass my criteria of some observation of interaction before I will enter into the picture. If people have not spoken to one of my trusted friends I do not feel that I can converse with them. This way, at worst, I blank someone who could be an acquaintance; at best, I prevent an embarrassing situation of talking out loud to a ghost that is only of my seeing and experience. Even if I know I am different it does not mean I want others to know that I am different.

At work I am my own person. I have a degree of control over how I manage my role. As long as I can fulfil the requirements, my methods and my time management, and to some extent people management, are there for my own manipulation. I feel trusted for what people see me as. They do not know an alternative side. This does create a pressure to conform to an expectation, but their expectation is one that I have created myself. My home made persona.

Nothing, however, can take away from the fact that I feel different and separate from other people on this planet. Maybe everyone feels this way but I have never heard it expressed before. I try hard to connect in many ways, to be accepted as me, but also know I will always be detached as that is my safety. That is my world.

I am beginning to understand that if I can learn to cope with the sensations that I experience, I could live with them. Hand in hand, mind in mind with the crazy world that I feel I exist in. It is time to stop fighting and to find a way of being part of this alternative world whilst also living a plausible life in the popular world today. I have choices much like any other being and my choice today must be to live as independently as possible but with a total awareness of my everyday differences. Because of my existence in different parameters I feel that when people talk about boundaries and self containment I struggle. My concept of boundaries is very internal and I find it difficult to judge how I fit in safely with different environments i.e. knowing when it is ok to say 'no', is a really difficult judgement for me to make. I have been talking about my lack of boundaries for many years and it is only dawning on me that I do have boundaries but I do not think they correspond with the majority in their existence.

I try to look after myself in my world but find it hard to impose this on the world at large. These overlaps and mismatches can make my life very uncomfortable as I constantly strive to please others regardless of boundaries and acceptability. The big world takes priority and my microcosm moulds around it.

Chapter 24

I feel at times like a Russian doll. Layers of being that go from the outer skin to the inner soul. To many it is vital that the outer layer is polished, bright and shiny. It is important to keep things together and to portray a happy togetherness of mind and body. What am I afraid of? The inside layers below skin deep, how I really feel true to myself. Even tentatively writing about this it is uncomfortable taking a risk to expose a vulnerable broken side.

Inside is dark and hollow. Negative feelings rattle around, sadness, despair, loneliness, isolation all come naturally to me – my primary feelings. It is the persistence of these inner feelings, my hot thoughts that make daily life at times a battle. What am I afraid of?

I go to work and enjoy it. I enjoy the challenge of working with clients, individuals, groups, colleagues – all a challenge when my inside demands isolation. I enjoy having responsibility and control – at least this is one area of my life that I can say that I have a vestige of control over successfully. If I let my inner feelings out however there is a fear that this responsibility and control would vanish I would not be able to function in a working environment and fit in with expectations. My want would be to wander off at times to give myself space to unwind rather than pushing on because that is what I demand in a working environment – to do my job to the best of my ability, and better. I am afraid of what would be left if I let people see the inside layers. No work, no meaning, no need to fight, all just for a shiny outer shell.

Why is it only skin deep? Why can't confidence penetrate any further that the outer layer? Sometimes I never know whether to start on the outside and try to cultivate it to go deeper the more I get to know and feel at home with a fake surface? Can I make the fake a reality? The alternative is to battle from the inside and challenge the depths to reinforce the fragile surface shell - build some roots? The difficulty is to confront the troubles within. I am not sure what I may find, although of course my natural predilection is negative, that is a daunting thought. What may I find? What if I drown in them? Is it better I function on the outside or is it the next step to go beyond the comfortable and push on further and deeper? So many questions and no idea about the answers – I am choosing to think about it today which may be the first step of many but thinking is as far as it goes at present. If I familiarise myself with the ideas I have written above they will not seem so insurmountable eventually (I hope) and then the process will be on the way. Tomorrow is always different. I always wish for tomorrow and to stay in the day is uncomfortable. I need to be distracted all of the time otherwise my discomfort leads to endless planning for the next time, the next day, the next year . . . To stay in the day is a challenge for me – that raises another question - What is the problem with today?

'It was only through my anxiety that I can participate in life, and for this reason I would not want to be without it'

Franz Kafka.

Chapter 25

The start of a work day.

Not too troublesome last night, only woke a couple of times which is normal. I don't particularly like nights as it is by nature a dark time and also a long time. I sleep with my husband, T, but he is in a world of dreams whilst I am wondering whether it is safe to get up to go to the bathroom or not. Whether it is OK that the three men standing in the corner of the bedroom are staring at me – they know I am awake. I have to go. I rush to the bathroom in the dark – no lights on as I do not want to attract attention to my journey. Then back to bed and all is a relief kicking my feet back under the duvet as quickly as possible as if there was a crocodile under the bed waiting to snap at a lingering toe. I lie there listening to my heart which lulls me back to some sense of peace.

The alarm, radio 5, blares out at 7am on a school day. I have to rush. The men are still in the corner – different men, same corner, but I do not have time to deliberate about them. At first there was no way of deciphering whether they were real or 'my people'. I then learnt that if I threw something at the offensive men they would disappear. This method was refined again when T suggested that I just waved a scarf at them so that I could see the scarf float through the air unimpeded by men who disappear. This took a lot of confidence though as I had to be close to the men to do this trick which despite its success never sat comfortably with me and I would always feel the fear approaching them. However, I was taught a new trick the other week where, if I shine a torch at my men they appear to be slightly translucent and ebb away – I can then get up without a concern (well sort of!). The torch has been a godsend to me and my morning routine as it has taken a big element of the unknown away. I never know who the men are but I do know they are there for me. I am not even totally sure of their motives any more as they have become a regular feature – but I do know that they don't like me and that is enough to place an element of risk in my mind about getting up in the mornings. I know I have to get to work by 7.30am though, this does not leave me a lot of free time to deliberate, so I must get on. This is one of the reasons why I leave myself a tight time schedule –no time to deliberate or panic – just get on.

I am up and into the bathroom. I quickly go under the shower, trying to identify my mood for the day. The weather usually helps in this process. If it is bright outside I am more likely to follow suit. If it is dull or gloomy in the morning then I have to get my self going and to be positive. To look at myself in the mirror is not my favourite pastime so it is done for purely functional reasons of on with the make up, slap some wax on wet hair and hope that things come together. No time to deliberate!

My clothes were chosen the night before and are usually hanging on the wardrobe door. I like to think about what I wear to school as my image is quite important. Last year at the staff Christmas Party I got an award in our department for the 'snappiest dresser' therefore I have a reputation to keep up. Bright colours and lots of jewellery. One of the students referred to me, to another member of staff, as the 'tall one with all the 'bling'!!' I like this as it is a positive identity within a large school of 1400 students and 140 teachers and staff. I like to choose my reasons for being known and not to be known for something I am not in control of.

I am dressed. T is still dreaming but I go to him to say my goodbye for the day. We kiss and he asks 'What time will you be back tonight?', the answer varies according to the day but it is usually 5.30pm or 6pm, with an early finish on Friday of 3pm. T promptly falls back to sleep again whilst I make my way downstairs. By this time our two basset hounds, Olive (a neurotic but loving Bassett Fauve) and Roxy (a big soft white Bassett Griffon Vendeen Grand) have woken up and are banging on the kitchen door to go out. It is a great greeting every morning to come down to excited wagging tails desperate for company and a run in the garden. I let them out and generally ignore them as I am still on my 30 minute schedule. On mornings when I am 'together' I try a bit of meditation in the kitchen comprising of some Reiki moves that my therapist Annie gave to me and also a method of covering my self in yellow and violet light from head to foot to protect myself during the day. I start by feeling the light in my hands and then I can see the golden presence. I carry it from above my head and slowly spread it down around my body to the floor covering all extremities. It feels good and warm and relaxing. I can see and feel the protection and I could spend much longer doing it but am glad for a snap shot visit first thing and promise myself that one day I will extend my time to get ready and fit in more meditation. Calm.

Then the next decision hits me – should I, or should I not eat a banana? This is a struggle for me as my default setting is to avoid food at all costs. A banana is about one hundred calories and is that going to break my balance of 1200 that I like to limit myself to in a day? Some days, most days, I just shove it in my bag and vow to myself I will eat it at school. Delay the decision. One thing that is a must is the taking of medication. I hate taking it but know I must to try to stay on track. A quick drink of orange juice straight from the carton – I hate doing that too but it has become a bad habit and a timesaving gesture. I have to prepare for my day ahead by grabbing one, or if I am feeling needy or decadent, two cans of diet coke for my day. The dogs are back in so it is a choice of shoes from about seven pairs that I have for school and then a quick cuddle with Roxy first and then Olive who looks forlorn as I am not staying. Grab keys and off to the door.

The cool air is refreshing and it is good to get out of the house in the morning – I feel like a person in my own right doing something that real people do such as going to work. It makes me feel grown up and important. In a world of fears and hang ups this interlude is bliss. I get to the car – black Nissan Note – and dump my bags of files and paperwork (plus one or two cans of diet coke) into the back seat trying not to scratch the paintwork with the keys. T only repaired it last week! The first thing that hits me is the music. Van Morrison is on at the moment very loud. It is great and clears the head. I then become aware of the time as the car starts and the clock flashes up – usually 7.23am. This is perfect timing as it is only a couple of miles to school. I could walk but have not done so in the last three and a half years of working there. The next seven minutes however can be fraught with danger and difficulty. In my life familiarity and routine can help but according to the voices in my head I hear that 'people' are 'after me' and want to kill me. I constantly hear a male aggressive voice telling me people are following me and want to kill me. I can only take this as the truth as I have heard it so often and in a very scary and angry voice shouting at me – I am frightened to dismiss it. If I think of questioning the voice he seems to know and gets more aggressive – it is like a battle in my head of my thoughts being shouted down by the aggression of the voice. I know there is nobody in the back seat of the car as I put my bags in there just a minute ago, but how do I know that I am not being watched? One help is to look up to the lounge window where my two dogs have their eyes trained on me. They are quiet so I must be alone. If anyone else was about they would be barking a welcome to them. I am safe.

The journey begins. Should I go uphill or downhill? I live half way up a hill and the routes to school either way are equidistant. Every morning I feel that I have to go a different route so it is harder for anyone following me to get familiar with my patterns. If I feel I am being followed I will automatically turn off and change direction. I always suffer from the sensation and belief of being followed. If I let it get under my skin I panic and have to go quicker. My heart races and the cold sweat gathers on my brow. The two miles to school can take the seven minutes and I rarely arrive after 7.30am but the journey is quite a stressful part of my morning which ends in relief at arriving at the school. I park the car. School does not start for the kids until 8.50am the place is fairly empty. I park in the same place every day in the corner of the car park overlooking the lacrosse pitches. I walk past the field into the school and down the art corridor to my department. My department is the Learning Support department which is upstairs. My room faces the top of the stairs and there is never anyone in the department there before me at that time in the morning. I unlock my office door and feel safe as I know anyone I see in there must be one of 'my people' that only I can see, as whoever locked the door last night would not have locked anyone in. No one has been in since so they must be my people. These days I also carry a small torch in my handbag so that I can detect 'my people'.

My first job in the empty office is to set the coffee percolator buzzing. The smell and taste of fresh coffee in the morning gets me going and tickles the senses. Coffee, especially strong varieties (with espresso being my favourite) goes straight to my head immediately leaving me feeling high and elated. The buzz is special and is something I crave. Caffeine is a big part of my morning and the mug of strong fresh coffee combined with my first can of diet coke gives me the gumption to carry on. At first it never used to be diet coke as well but as time progresses I need more! That is why the question of one

ЛLucy

or two cans has to be broached every morning before I leave the kitchen. I used to make one can last all morning and just drink coffee in the afternoon. Now I need a whole can and a coffee to kick start me first thing and then another can accompanied by copious amounts of coffee to span the morning schedule. What did I do without it?

Usually one more thing before other staff members appear and that is to check my pigeon hole box. I look out for notes written in thick black pen which always come from our Head of Department, she is quite demanding but runs a good department which we are all proud to be part of. The children come first and it is always a department where they are welcome. School life can be a mine field of difficulties, especially as this particular school is a high achieving and demanding establishment. The range of students accessing Learning Support and emotional nourishment come from across the age ranges of the school and with no regard to social standing or intellectual gifts. We are a strong team of about twenty five individuals who unite against the plethora of black pen notes that get left for us!

There is nothing left to hold back time, I watch breakfast for the boarding students, of whom there are about one hundred and twenty in number from various backgrounds and countries. It is unusual at our school as it is a state school with a system of fee paying boarders paying only for the boarding element whilst accessing the non fee paying education on offer. The balance is a really successful one and places are at a premium. I often wonder about their life in the school, alongside my need to escape the school every evening at the close of my duties. It is morning though and I need to focus on my day ahead. I look forward to working with students but sometimes get tangled up in administration and paperwork. My anticipation for the day however is positive and the knowledge that I will be non stop all day without a minute to stop and worry helps me to cope with the forthcoming onslaught. I love it but it is stressful and tests my resilience at times on each and every day. I am determined however to live up to that 'grown up' feeling that I experienced leaving the house an hour ago, and will do my best not to let the 'others' get the better of me.

ANOTHER DAY AND FURTHER BATTLES BEGIN.

I WILL SURVIVE

Acknowledgements

My thanks to my husband T for typing, correcting and advising in the writing of this book.

Thanks also to my many friends who have put up with my strange actions without knowing the full story.

About The Author

The author has a degree at Loughborough University, with a 2:1 in Psychology.

She has played International tennis.

She has a Masters Degree in Forensic and Legal Psychology.

She worked with drug and alcohol users as a qualified counsellor psychotherapist.

She has for the past 5 years been working as a school counsellor, with children aged between 11 and 17 years of age.

Lightning Source UK Ltd.
Milton Keynes UK
UKOW04f2243180913

217478UK00001B/36/P